MATH
WEEKLY PRACTICE
Grade 5

Credits
Author: Redeana Davis Smith
Copy Editor: Elise Craver

Visit *carsondellosa.com* for correlations to Common Core, state, national, and Canadian provincial standards.

Carson-Dellosa Publishing, LLC
PO Box 35665
Greensboro, NC 27425 USA
carsondellosa.com

978-1-4838-2799-5
01-053167784

Table of Contents

Introduction

The Weekly Practice series provides 40 weeks of essential daily practice in either math or language arts. It is the perfect supplement to any classroom curriculum and provides standards-based activities for every day of the week but Friday.

The activities are intended as homework assignments for Monday through Thursday and cover a wide spectrum of standards-based skills. The skills are presented at random to provide comprehensive learning but are repeated systematically throughout the book. The intention is to offer regular, focused practice to ensure mastery and retention.

Each 192-page book provides 40 weeks of reproducible pages, a standards alignment matrix, flash cards, and an answer key. The reproducible pages are perfect for homework but also work well for morning work, early finishers, and warm-up activities.

About This Book

Each page contains a variety of short, fun exercises that build in difficulty across the span of the book. The activities are divided into two sections:

- The Daily Extension Activities at the front of the book are intended to engage both student and family. These off-the-page activities are simple and fun so that students will look forward to this practice time at home. The activities span one week at a time. The instructions are clear and simple so that students can follow them with or without assistance in their homes. None need be returned to school.

- The daily practice section involves more comprehensive learning. Because of the simplicity of directions and straightforward tasks, students will be able to complete most tasks independently in a short period of time. There are four pages of activities per week, allowing for testing or a student break on Friday if desired. These pages are intended to be brought back to school.

Pages can be offered in any order, making it possible to reinforce specific skills when needed. However, skills are repeated regularly throughout the book to ensure retention over time, making a strong case for using pages sequentially.

An answer key is included for the daily practice section. You can check answers as a group for a quick follow-up lesson or monitor students' progress individually. Follow the basic page layout provided at the beginning of the answer key to match answers to page placement. Also included in the book is a set of flash cards. Reproduce them to give to students for at-home practice, or place them in classroom centers.

Common Core State Standards
Alignment Matrix

Standard	W1	W2	W3	W4	W5	W6	W7	W8	W9	W10	W11	W12	W13	W14	W15	W16	W17	W18	W19	W20
5.OA.A.1	•		•	•	•	•	•	•	•	•			•		•		•		•	
5.OA.A.2		•	•	•		•		•		•		•	•	•	•	•		•		•
5.OA.B.3	•	•	•		•		•	•	•	•	•	•	•	•	•	•	•	•	•	•
5.NBT.A.1	•	•	•	•	•		•		•		•	•	•		•		•	•	•	•
5.NBT.A.2	•	•	•	•	•	•	•	•	•	•	•	•	•	•	•	•	•	•	•	•
5.NBT.A.3	•	•	•	•	•	•	•	•	•	•	•	•	•	•	•	•	•	•	•	•
5.NBT.A.4	•	•	•	•	•	•	•	•	•	•	•	•	•	•	•	•	•	•	•	•
5.NBT.B.5	•			•			•			•		•	•	•	•	•	•	•	•	•
5.NBT.B.6			•				•				•	•	•	•	•	•	•	•	•	•
5.NBT.B.7	•	•	•	•	•	•	•	•	•		•	•	•	•	•	•	•	•	•	•
5.NF.A.1	•	•	•	•	•	•	•	•	•	•	•	•	•	•	•	•	•	•	•	•
5.NF.A.2		•		•		•		•	•	•	•	•	•	•	•	•	•		•	•
5.NF.B.3				•								•		•	•			•		•
5.NF.B.4							•	•						•		•			•	•
5.NF.B.5							•		•			•								
5.NF.B.6			•			•		•			•				•		•	•	•	•
5.NF.B.7	•																			•
5.MD.A.1	•	•	•	•	•	•	•	•	•	•		•	•	•	•	•	•	•	•	
5.MD.B.2				•		•	•	•	•	•										
5.MD.C.3																		•		
5.MD.C.4																				
5.MD.C.5																				
5.G.A.1	•	•	•	•	•		•		•		•							•		
5.G.A.2											•		•		•		•		•	
5.G.B.3	•	•	•	•	•								•	•					•	
5.G.B.4		•				•	•	•	•	•	•	•	•	•	•	•	•	•	•	•

W = Week

Common Core State Standards Alignment Matrix

Standard	W21	W22	W23	W24	W25	W26	W27	W28	W29	W30	W31	W32	W33	W34	W35	W36	W37	W38	W39	W40
5.OA.A.1	●	●	●		●		●		●		●		●		●		●	●	●	●
5.OA.A.2		●		●	●	●		●		●		●		●		●		●	●	●
5.OA.B.3	●	●	●	●	●	●	●	●	●	●	●	●	●	●	●	●	●	●	●	●
5.NBT.A.1	●				●	●	●		●		●		●		●		●		●	
5.NBT.A.2	●	●	●	●	●	●	●	●	●	●	●	●	●	●	●	●	●	●	●	●
5.NBT.A.3	●	●	●	●	●	●	●	●	●	●	●	●	●	●	●	●	●	●	●	●
5.NBT.A.4	●		●		●		●		●	●	●	●	●		●		●		●	
5.NBT.B.5	●	●	●	●	●	●	●	●	●	●	●	●	●	●	●	●	●	●	●	●
5.NBT.B.6		●	●	●		●	●	●		●	●	●		●	●	●		●	●	●
5.NBT.B.7	●	●	●	●	●	●	●	●	●	●	●	●	●	●	●	●	●	●	●	●
5.NF.A.1	●	●	●	●	●	●	●	●	●	●	●	●	●	●	●	●	●	●	●	●
5.NF.A.2		●	●	●	●	●	●	●	●	●	●	●	●	●	●	●	●		●	●
5.NF.B.3		●	●		●	●	●	●		●	●	●		●		●		●		●
5.NF.B.4	●	●	●	●	●		●	●	●	●	●	●	●	●	●	●	●	●	●	●
5.NF.B.5	●	●	●	●	●	●		●	●	●				●						
5.NF.B.6		●		●	●	●		●		●		●	●		●	●	●	●	●	●
5.NF.B.7				●					●	●	●	●	●	●	●	●	●	●	●	●
5.MD.A.1	●	●	●	●	●	●	●	●	●	●	●	●	●	●	●	●	●	●	●	●
5.MD.B.2			●				●											●		
5.MD.C.3					●									●	●		●			
5.MD.C.4						●	●	●	●	●	●	●	●	●						
5.MD.C.5									●	●	●	●	●	●	●	●	●	●	●	●
5.G.A.1	●	●		●								●		●			●		●	
5.G.A.2		●			●		●		●											
5.G.B.3		●		●	●	●		●		●			●	●	●		●	●	●	●
5.G.B.4	●		●						●		●				●					

W = Week

School to Home Communication

The research is clear that family involvement is strongly linked to student success. Support for student learning at home improves student achievement in school. Educators should not underestimate the significance of this connection.

The activities in this book create an opportunity to create or improve this school-to-home link. The activities span a week at a time and can be sent home as a week-long homework packet each Monday. Simply clip together the strip of fun activities from the front of the book with the pages for Days 1 to 4 for the correct week.

Most of the activities can be completed independently, but many encourage feedback or interaction with a family member. The activities are simple and fun, aiming to create a brief pocket of learning that is enjoyable to all.

In order to make the school-to-home program work for students and their families, we encourage you to reach out to them with an introductory letter. Explain the program and its intent and ask them to partner with you in their children's educational process. Describe the role you expect them to play. Encourage them to offer suggestions or feedback along the way.

A sample letter is included below. Use it as is or create your own letter to introduce this project and elicit their collaboration.

Dear Families,

I anticipate a productive and exciting year of learning and look forward to working with you and your child. We have a lot of work to do! I hope we—teacher, student, and family—can work together as a team to achieve the goal of academic progress we all hope for this year.

I will send home a packet of homework each week on _____. There will be two items to complete each day: a single task on a strip plus a full page of focused practice. Each page or strip is labeled Day 1 (for Monday), Day 2, Day 3, or Day 4. There is no homework on Friday.

Please make sure that your student brings back the completed work _____. It is important that these are brought in on time as we may work on some of the lessons as a class.

If you have any questions about this program or would like to talk to me about it, please feel free to call or email me. Thank you for joining me in making this the best year ever for your student!

Sincerely,

_____

_____

_____

	Day 1	Day 2	Day 3	Day 4
Week 1	Look around your home and find two examples of parallel lines. How do you know they are parallel?	Find at least one pattern in your home. Discuss each pattern and what would come next.	Find some spare change and find the total amount. How much more do you need to reach $1.00? $5.00?	See how many different objects you can find that are shaped like a quadrilateral.

	Day 1	Day 2	Day 3	Day 4
Week 2	Do you have any pets? Place an *X* on a line plot to show how many pets you have. Think about other families you know and add their data to the line plot.	Gather measurement tools from around the house. Discuss ways each is used. Look closely at the related ones and explain how they are alike and different.	Create examples and non-examples of parallel lines with objects around your home, such as straws or belts.	Find two objects and compare their weights. Estimate how much you think each weighs.

	Day 1	Day 2	Day 3	Day 4
Week 3	Look around your home and find two examples of intersecting lines. How do you know they are intersecting?	See how many different examples of a right triangle you can find in your home.	Explore your home for symmetrical designs. How do you know they are symmetrical? Use a piece of yarn or string to show the line or lines of symmetry.	Estimate the perimeter of a room in your home. What unit of measurement did you choose? Why?

	Day 1	Day 2	Day 3	Day 4
Week 4	Look around your home and find two examples of perpendicular lines. How do you know they are perpendicular?	Arrange yourself and others in your family in height order. Estimate how tall everyone is. Estimate the differences between heights.	Find several 3-digit numbers in books, magazines, newspapers, or the mail. Discuss the value of each digit.	Discuss the order of operations. What operation do you do first? Last? What could happen if it is not followed when solving an equation?

	Day 1	Day 2	Day 3	Day 4
Week 5	Fold a piece of paper in half. Have a family member draw a design on one side using the fold as the line of symmetry. Then, draw the matching half on the other side.	Look at the clock nearest to you. What time will it be in two and a half hours?	Find an object that is about a meter long.	Describe the difference between multiplication and division.

	Day 1	Day 2	Day 3	Day 4
Week 6	Draw several different quadrilaterals. Discuss the similarities and differences between them.	Discuss what it means to have a remainder in a division problem.	What is a benchmark number? Discuss why one-half is considered a benchmark number.	Estimate how far you live from the nearest store. What unit of measurement did you choose? Why?

	Day 1	Day 2	Day 3	Day 4
Week 7	Find a small object. Turn it 270° clockwise. Then, turn it 270° counterclockwise. Talk about the differences between the rotations.	Fold a piece of paper in half. Explain how you know each side is half of the original whole.	Discuss what a fraction is. Then, discuss what a decimal is. How are they similar?	Find an object that you think weighs about five pounds. Can you find an object that weighs about twice as much? Explain your reasoning.

	Day 1	Day 2	Day 3	Day 4
Week 8	How many right angles can you find around your house? How do you know they are right angles?	Describe what happens to a number when it is multiplied by 10.	Think of three examples where multiplication is needed to solve real-world problems.	List the different ways fractions are used in the kitchen.

	Day 1	Day 2	Day 3	Day 4
Week 9	Discuss how you could find the perimeter of your home. What unit of measurement would you choose and why?	Create a pie chart showing how you spend a typical day. Estimate what fraction of the day you spend at school.	Think of three examples where decimals are used to solve real-world problems. Explain why decimals are used.	Look at your favorite recipe. Discuss how the measurements would change if you doubled the recipe.

	Day 1	Day 2	Day 3	Day 4
Week 10	Find as many different rectangles in your home as possible. Discuss the properties they all share.	Pick a sport. Brainstorm and list all of the different ways math is used in that sport.	Describe how comparing decimals in a grocery store could help you save money.	Discuss what an exponent is (i.e. the 2 in 10^2). Have you ever seen an exponent used outside of math class? Where?

	Day 1	Day 2	Day 3	Day 4
Week 11	Find as many examples of isosceles triangles as you can. Discuss the properties of isosceles triangles. How are they different from other types of triangles?	Look at the clock. What time is it? Round to the nearest half hour.	Find one object that you think weighs about a pound. How many ounces do you think it weighs?	Discuss how you could find the area of a room in your home. What unit of measurement would you use? Why?

	Day 1	Day 2	Day 3	Day 4
Week 12	Why do you think knowing math facts is important? Think of real-world examples to support your answer.	Find a collection of something in your home. Sort and count the collection. What properties did you use to sort?	Explain why it is useful to know the relationship between a kilogram and a gram.	Find three objects and put them in order from least to greatest weight.

	Day 1	Day 2	Day 3	Day 4
Week 13	Find an object that is about one yard long. Estimate how many inches long it is.	Work with a family member to find out how many miles you travel to and from school each week.	Fold a piece of paper in half, and then in half again. Color one section. What fraction did you shade?	Find out how much you weighed when you were born. How does that compare to your weight today? About how many times more do you weigh now?
Week 14	Estimate how much liquid you drink each day. Which unit of measure did you choose to use and why?	Find a receipt. Calculate how much the bill would have been if you doubled everything that was purchased.	Find an object that you think weighs twice as much as another object. Estimate how much each object weighs.	Find two containers holding something liquid. Estimate the capacity of both.
Week 15	See how many examples of right triangles you can find. Discuss the properties of a right triangle.	Would you rather have $\frac{57}{100}$ of a dollar or $\frac{6}{10}$ of a dollar? Explain.	Draw a rhombus and a square. Discuss the properties of each with your family. How are they the same? How are they different?	Find a way to mark and measure your height and the height of a family member. Compare the two heights.
Week 16	Where have you seen numbers in word form in real life? Why do you think it is important to be able to read and write numbers?	How many clocks do you have in your home? Make a graph showing how many are digital or analog.	Check the odometer on a vehicle. Round the mileage to the nearest hundred.	Create a line plot showing how many shoes each person in your home has.

10

	Day 1	Day 2	Day 3	Day 4
Week 17	Look around your house to find numbers (i.e. food packages, signs). Round those numbers to the highest place value.	Write your age as a fraction (for example, I'm 11 and $\frac{5}{6}$ years old). Do the same for one other person. What's the difference in your ages?	Find an object that would best be measured in centimeters. Estimate the length.	Find your heart rate by counting your pulse for 10 seconds and then multiplying by 6. Explain why you multiply by 6.
Week 18	Compare $\frac{3}{4}$ and $\frac{4}{5}$. Discuss which is larger and how you know.	Draw the face of a clock. Divide it into thirds. How many minutes are in one third of an hour?	Estimate the width of your front door in feet. Measure to see how close you were.	Share your favorite recipe. Discuss how the measurements would change if it were cut in half.
Week 19	See how many different polygons you can identify around your home.	Find as many acute angles as you can around your home. How do you know they are acute? What tool could you use to find out if you don't have a protractor?	Find a container holding liquid. See if the capacity is written on the container. How much liquid do you think is left?	Which room in your house has the largest area? Which unit of measurement would you use to find out?
Week 20	Find a receipt. If you had a coupon for $\frac{1}{10}$ off, how much would you have saved?	Find as many obtuse angles as you can. How do you know they are obtuse?	Time how long it takes you to eat dinner. If you spend that much time eating dinner every day, how much do you spend eating dinner in a week?	Fill three glasses equally with water. How much would you have to use from each glass to make four equal glasses?

	Day 1	Day 2	Day 3	Day 4
Week 21	Find three labeled food items and order them by their labeled weights.	Draw a variety of polygons on a piece of paper. Ask a family member to identify all of the polygons with parallel sides.	How many hours are in one week? How do you know? Find out the time you spend sleeping each week as a fraction.	Find two items in your home that weigh about a gram.
Week 22	Find a door and open it to a 45° angle. What would it look like if it were opened at a 90° angle?	How many acute angles can you find around your house? Estimate the measure of each.	Find an object that you think weighs about $\frac{1}{10}$ your weight. Explain your reasoning.	If you had a pizza for dinner shared equally among everyone in your home, what fraction of the pizza would you get? Explain.
Week 23	Find five books in your home. Estimate the weight of each and put them in order from lightest to heaviest.	Place a pencil on a flat surface. Rotate it 360° clockwise. Then, rotate it 360° counterclockwise. Discuss what you notice.	Create a line plot showing how many pillows are in each room of your home.	Find objects in your house that are arrays. How could arrays help you find the quantity without counting individual items?
Week 24	Do you have any doors in your house that can open greater than 90°? If so, estimate the angle measure of the widest they can open.	When dividing by powers of 10, which direction do you move the decimal? Discuss your answer and reasoning.	Fold a piece of paper into eighths. Is there more than one way to fold a paper into eighths? Discuss.	Find a book and find out how many pages it has. Estimate which page would be exactly halfway through the book. Then, calculate where the halfway point really is.

	Day 1	Day 2	Day 3	Day 4
Week 25	Find examples of equilateral triangles around your house. How do you know they are equilateral triangles?	Write an expression showing the number of doorknobs in your home less 3.	Find 12 small objects. Discuss the different ways you could sort them. Then, divide them evenly into four groups.	If you go to bed tonight at 8:30 pm and sleep for $10\frac{1}{4}$ hours, what time will you wake up?

	Day 1	Day 2	Day 3	Day 4
Week 26	Find five objects that would not be classified as polygons. Discuss the reasons why.	If each person in your family won $5.55, how much did your family win in all? Discuss the different combinations of bills and coins you could be paid in.	Write out the steps that would help a neighbor find the volume of her rectangular pool.	Find a favorite recipe. Discuss how you would change the measurements if you tripled the recipe.

	Day 1	Day 2	Day 3	Day 4
Week 27	Find an example of a trapezoid. Discuss the properties that make it a trapezoid.	If you shared $\frac{1}{3}$ of a pizza with a family member, how much of the original pizza would you each get? Explain with pictures.	Find a rectangular prism, such as a tissue box. Estimate the volume of the prism. Explain the unit of measurement you chose.	Estimate the length of your foot. Compare the length to others' feet. Estimate the total length if you added all of your family's feet together.

	Day 1	Day 2	Day 3	Day 4
Week 28	Fold a paper into fourths. Then, fold it into eighths. Discuss equivalent fractions using your paper.	Discuss what happens to a number when it is divided by 10. Describe any patterns that you see.	Find two prisms that have different dimensions but would have similar volume. Discuss why this is possible.	Write an expression for twice the number of windows in your home.

	Day 1	Day 2	Day 3	Day 4
Week 29	Find a rectangular prism. Estimate the volume. Find another prism that has about half the volume.	Draw a picture to show how you would share half of a pie between you and two others.	Mark one side of a room as 0 and the other as 1. Call out fractions and stand at the appropriate place on the "number line."	Find an empty container. Experiment with filling it $\frac{1}{2}$ full, $\frac{3}{4}$ full, $\frac{1}{3}$ full, etc. How do you know it is filled to about that fraction?

	Day 1	Day 2	Day 3	Day 4
Week 30	Find examples of scalene triangles around your house. Discuss the properties of a scalene triangle.	Draw a clock face. Divide the face into sixths. How many minutes are in a sixth of an hour? How do you know?	Draw a picture to prove or disprove the following. $\frac{2}{3} = \frac{4}{6}$	Discuss what it means to estimate. When might someone need to use estimation to solve real-world problems?

	Day 1	Day 2	Day 3	Day 4
Week 31	Find three different types of triangles around your house. Discuss their similarities and differences.	A gallon of ice cream is shared evenly among 8 people. Express how much each person would get without using a fraction.	Find a handful of spare change. Count the coins. Round to the nearest tenth of a dollar.	Discuss how you would find out how many square feet of carpet to purchase if you were putting carpet down in a room of your choice.

	Day 1	Day 2	Day 3	Day 4
Week 32	Find two coins. Add to find their total value and write it as a fraction.	Write a few sentences explaining why 0.25 and $\frac{1}{4}$ are equivalent. Include pictures or models as needed.	Draw a diagram with directions explaining how to find the volume of one room in your home.	Think of three examples in which volume can be used to solve real-world problems.

	Day 1	Day 2	Day 3	Day 4
Week 33	Create a picture using only polygons. Make it a family affair and have everyone add to the picture.	"Hide" points on a coordinate plane. Have someone call out coordinates to try and find your hidden points.	Estimate the length and width of a window in your home. What unit of measurement would you use and why?	Find three objects that are about 1 foot each in length. Combine them end to end. Discuss the new length. Can you convert it to a larger unit?
Week 34	Play "I Spy" with someone by identifying different polygons. For example, "I spy a polygon with…"	Draw a clock face. Divide the face into fifths. How many minutes are there in $\frac{1}{5}$ of an hour?	Sketch a cube with a volume of 125 cubic units. Explain how you know its dimensions.	Sketch several different possible dimensions of a backyard with an area of 240 square feet.
Week 35	Estimate the lengths of 6 items. Sort them from shortest to longest. What unit of measurement did you use? Why?	Sketch a coordinate plane. Plot and record the ordered pairs needed to create a trapezoid in the first quadrant.	Write a note explaining how you can use a 1 cup measuring cup to add 2 pints of milk to a bowl for a recipe.	Find as many different kitchen measuring instruments as possible. Sort them from smallest to largest.
Week 36	Would you rather have $\frac{1}{4}$ of $100 or $\frac{1}{2}$ of $60? Explain your reasoning.	As a family, create a story problem for $3 \div \frac{1}{2}$.	Find an object that is about 1 inch long. About how many of the object would it take to measure 1 yard? How do you know?	Draw the different possibile dimensions of a rug that measures 48 square feet.

	Day 1	Day 2	Day 3	Day 4
Week 37	Estimate the length of your bed. What unit of measurement did you choose? Why?	When multiplying by powers of 10, which direction does the decimal move? Explain why.	Fold a piece of paper into sixteenths. Use it to prove or disprove the following comparison. $\frac{1}{4} > \frac{3}{16}$	Create riddles with coins. Choose a few coins and tell someone "I have 4 coins that are worth ___." Switch roles and repeat.

	Day 1	Day 2	Day 3	Day 4
Week 38	Show five different ways of illustrating $\frac{1}{2}$. Explain.	Write a note convincing someone that $\frac{3}{4}$ is equivalent to 0.75. Include models as needed.	Teach someone what you know about the order of operations. List the steps in order.	Explain why a 3-yard by 3-yard area rug and a 9-foot by 9-foot area rug are the same.

	Day 1	Day 2	Day 3	Day 4
Week 39	Sketch a regular and an irregular hexagon. List the similarities and differences between the two hexagons.	Visualize a room as a coordinate plane. If possible, use painter's tape to show the axes on the floor. Call out ordered pairs and move to plot yourself on the plane.	Mark one side of a room as 0 and the other as 1. Call out decimals and stand at the appropriate place on the "number line."	Draw a rectangular yard that has an area of 720 square feet. Label the dimensions.

	Day 1	Day 2	Day 3	Day 4
Week 40	Write a note to convince someone that a square can also be a rectangle. Be sure to refer to the properties of each.	Explain to someone why 6 dimes is the same as 60 pennies. Write them both as fractions and decimals to illustrate.	Calculate how many hours on a typical weekday you spend at home. Represent this amount as a fraction.	Calculate how many copies of you it would take to weigh a ton. Explain your answer.

Draw a set of parallel lines.

Write the number.

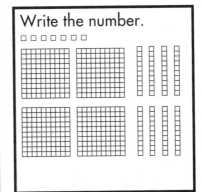

0, 10, 20, 30, 40, ...

Rule _____

Complete the drawing using the dotted line as the line of symmetry.

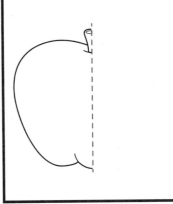

What time will it be in three and a half hours?

_____

Plot the points on the coordinate plane.
(2, 3), (2, 5), (5, 3), (5, 5)

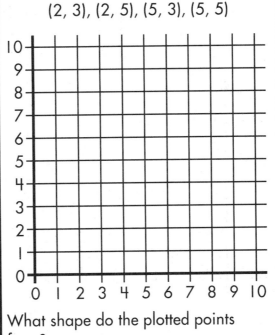

What shape do the plotted points form? _____

Write 2.54 in word form.

7 x 3,000 = _____

7 x ✦ = 42

42 ÷ 6 = ✦

Draw a check on the triangles and circle the quadrilaterals.

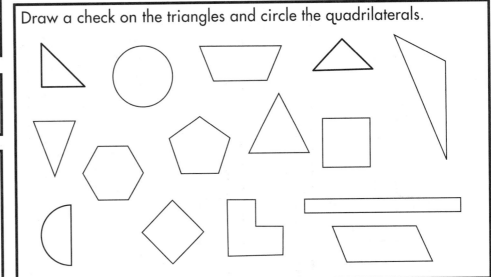

Name _____

Write the number.

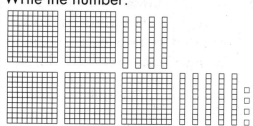

Draw the fractions.

$\dfrac{2}{6}$ ◯

$\dfrac{1}{2}$ ◯

$\dfrac{6}{12}$ ◯

What is the value of y in the equation?

$32.53 - y = 14.28$

◯ 17.25

◯ 18.36

◯ 18.25

◯ 19.47

Solve. What patterns do you see?

9 × 5 = _____	4 × 3 = _____
90 × 5 = _____	40 × 3 = _____
900 × 5 = _____	400 × 3 = _____
8 × 7 = _____	6 × 2 = _____
80 × 7 = _____	60 × 2 = _____
800 × 7 = _____	600 × 2 = _____

$$\begin{array}{r} 342.20 \\ -\ 23.64 \\ \hline \end{array}$$

What is the value of the 7 in 738?

Which expression means "add 430 and 44, then multiply by 8"?

◯ 8 + (430 + 44)

◯ 8 × (430 + 44)

◯ 8 − (430 − 44)

◯ 8 ÷ (430 + 44)

Rule: Add 3

3, 6, _____, _____, _____

Evaluate the numerical expression.

(9 − 2) × 4

Plot the points on the coordinate plane.

A (2, 3)   **B** (2, 5)
C (5, 3)   **D** (5, 5)

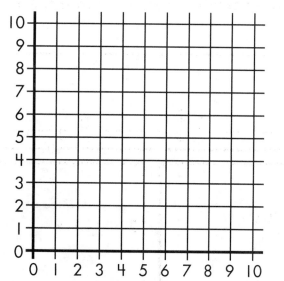

18

Write the decimals. Compare the numbers.

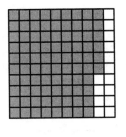 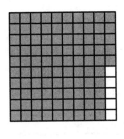

_____ _____

In which number is the value of the digit in the thousands place ten times as much as the value of the digit in the hundreds place?

◯ 23,433

◯ 12,287

◯ 123,456

◯ 46,778

Word Form

728.29

Hundreds	Tens	Ones	Tenths	Hundredths

Expanded Form

1 ton = _____ pounds

Shade $\frac{1}{2}$.

Which is the correct sum?

2.43 + 1.8

◯ 3.3

◯ 4.33

◯ 2.51

◯ 4.23

Place each fraction on the number line. Then, round each to the nearest whole number.

0   1

A. $\frac{1}{3}$ _____ B. $\frac{3}{3}$ _____ C. $\frac{2}{3}$ _____ D. $\frac{0}{3}$ _____

Write as a decimal.

seven tenths

7 × 111 =

Write the number.

Complete the chart using the rules.

Rule: +3	x	2					
Rule: +5	y	2					

I minute is _____ times as long as I second.

What is the value and place of the underlined digit?

5<u>2</u>5.5	20	tens
33<u>2</u>.57	_____	_____
137.1<u>2</u>5	_____	_____
<u>6</u>32.924	_____	_____
345.<u>3</u>6	_____	_____
42.47<u>1</u>	_____	_____

If Bert rounds each item to the nearest dollar, about how much will he spend at the store?

Bert's Grocery List

Bananas....$1.98

Bread.....$2.32

Milk.....$2.58

Eggs....$1.49

0.5 ◯ 0.75

5,090
+ 283

Identify each shape. Write its name inside the shape.

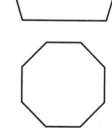

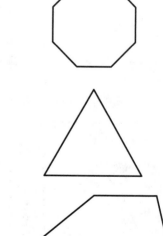

21
× 9

Which is a composite number?

◯ 19

◯ 7

◯ 21

◯ 5

Write the number.

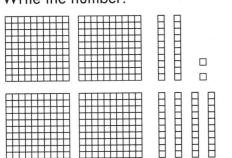

Draw a line with end points A and B.

$\frac{1}{2}$ ◯ $\frac{1}{3}$

Each of my five sides are congruent. What am I?

Draw me.

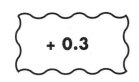

+ 0.3

0.2 ⟹ _____

1.4 ⟹ _____

3.2 ⟹ _____

2.7 ⟹ _____

0.4 ⟹ _____

4.5 ⟹ _____

7.6 ⟹ _____

5.3 ⟹ _____

```
              X
  X           X
  X           X        X
  X     X     X        X
  X     X     X        X
  0     1     2     3     4
```

Number of Pets

How many students in the class have exactly 4 pets?

Write as a decimal.
Three and forty-five hundredths

5,000 × 9 = _____

Color the circles that are greater than 0.60.

(0.4)   (0.19)   (0.88)   (0.39)   (0.28)

(0.06)   (0.61)   (0.48)   (0.68)   (0.5)

(0.7)   (0.59)   (0.08)   (0.53)   (0.9)

7 × = 56

⬡ ÷ 7 = 8

The last time it was measured, the class's pet snake was 1 foot 7 inches long. How many inches long was the snake?

Nellie baked muffins for her family. She thought that she put the same amount of batter in each cup, but the muffins are all different heights. Put the muffins in order from shortest to tallest.

2.14 in., 1.98 in.,
2.12 in., 2.05 in.

Victor says he has about $4.00. Is he correct? Why or why not?

Find the pattern to complete the ordered pairs.

(1, 6)

(3, 18)

(5, 30)

(_____, _____)

(_____, _____)

$$\begin{array}{r} 24.39 \\ + 42.84 \\ \hline \end{array}$$

$$\begin{array}{r} \frac{1}{2} \\ + \frac{3}{4} \\ \hline \end{array}$$

Oscar bought a pair of pants for $17.89, a shirt for $12.49, and a pair of shoes for $22.73. About how much did Oscar spend? Round to the nearest dollar.

Name the ordered pair at each point.

A _____   B _____

C _____   D _____

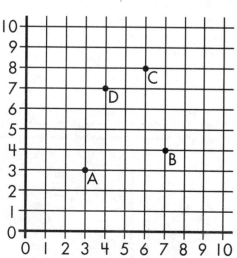

Rule: Multiply by 10

10, _____, _____, _____, _____

Write an equation for the story.
Nadia has three times as many trading cards as Marcella.

22

I have one set of parallel lines. My angles add up to 360°. None of my angles or lines have to be congruent. What shape am I?

_____

I have two sets of parallel lines. Each set of lines is congruent. My angles add up to 360°. My opposite angles are congruent. What shape am I?

_____

In which number is the value of the digit in the tens place one-tenth the value of the digit in the hundreds place?

○ 35,629

○ 33,479

○ 90,454

○ 34,885

Word Form

315.89

Hundreds	Tens	Ones	Tenths	Hundredths

Expanded Form

15 qt. ◯ 4 gal.

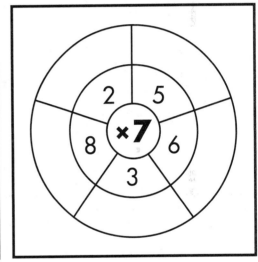

2,358.82
+ 987.38

Round the answer to nearest hundred.

_____

Complete the fractions so they are equivalent to $\frac{1}{2}$.

$\frac{\_}{10}$ $\frac{2}{\_}$ $\frac{\_}{20}$ $\frac{\_}{18}$

$\frac{\_}{8}$ $\frac{\_}{14}$ $\frac{6}{\_}$

7.863

Round to the nearest

hundredth. _____

tenth. _____

whole number. _____

Make the smallest whole number possible using all 6 digits.

3, 9, 4, 8, 2, 5

The scales showed 3.429 pounds when Jenna weighed her grapes at the grocery store. What is the weight of the grapes rounded to the nearest tenth?

○ 3.43 lb.   ○ 3.5 lb.

○ 3.4 lb.   ○ 3 lb.

List the metric unit you would use to measure the length of each object.

table _____

bug _____

road _____

cabinet _____

hand span _____

Write an expression for 15 more than b.

Kyra ran $\frac{3}{8}$ of a mile on Monday and $\frac{1}{4}$ of a mile on Tuesday. How much did she run in all?

The grocer packs three bags of produce in one box. The bag of apples weighs 3.46 pounds. The bag of oranges weighs 2.83 pounds and the bag of plums weighs 1.41 pounds. How much did the box of produce weigh?

0.01 ◯ 0.1

$4.78
+ $3.24

The main sail on Thomas's sailboat was triangular. Its sides measured 12 feet, 15.5 feet, and 12 feet. What type of triangle was Thomas's sail?

○ scalene

○ equilateral

○ isosceles

200.02
− 157.33

How many 3-inch-long pieces can John cut from a board that is 2 yards long?

Draw a pair of intersecting lines that are not perpendicular.

$\dfrac{7}{8} - \dfrac{2}{8} =$ _____

$\dfrac{5}{6} - \dfrac{1}{6} =$ _____

$\dfrac{3}{4} - \dfrac{1}{4} =$ _____

$\dfrac{7}{10} - \dfrac{5}{10} =$ _____

4, 8, 12, 16, 20, ...

Rule _____

Identify each shape. Write its name inside the shape.

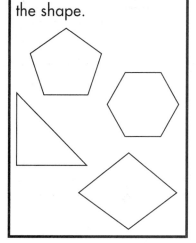

Solve for n.

$n = 5$

$6 + (n \div 1) =$

$20 - (n \div 5) =$

$(n + 15) \div 4 =$

Draw a coordinate plane. Label the x-axis, the y-axis, and the origin.

Write 32.81 in word form.

$3 \times 5,000 =$ _____

$4 \times$ ✦ $= 32$

$32 \div 8 =$ ✦

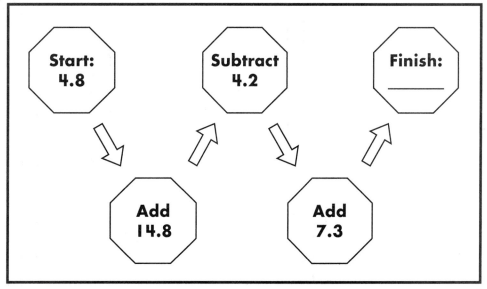

Start: 4.8

Subtract 4.2

Finish: _____

Add 14.8

Add 7.3

What is the remainder when 337 is divided by 5?

○ 7   ○ 1   ○ 3   ○ 2

Solve. What patterns do you see?

45 ÷ 5 = _____	12 ÷ 4 = _____
450 ÷ 5 = _____	120 ÷ 4 = _____
4,500 ÷ 5 = _____	1,200 ÷ 4 = _____
56 ÷ 8 = _____	12 ÷ 2 = _____
560 ÷ 8 = _____	120 ÷ 2 = _____
5,600 ÷ 8 = _____	1,200 ÷ 2 = _____

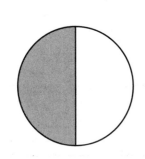

Write the shaded part as a decimal and a fraction.

fraction _____

decimal _____

What time will it be in $2\frac{1}{2}$ hours?

_____

456.87
+ 12.8
_____

What is the value of the 2 in 2,473?

Which of the following is not true?

○ 2.80 < 2.9

○ 2.88 = 2.8

○ 2.800 < 2.9

○ 2.08 > 2.008

Rule: Add 5

5, 10, _____, _____, _____

Evaluate the numerical expression.

15 + (3 × 6)

Plot the points on the coordinate plane.

A (1, 3)   **B** (3, 1)
C (5, 6)   **D** (6, 4)

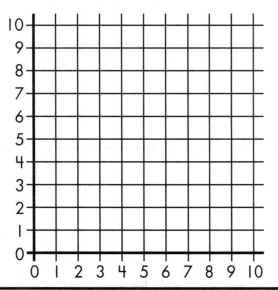

Name _____

Week 3, Day 3

Shade to represent 1.49.

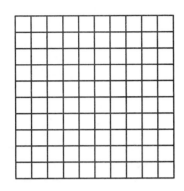

Which decimal rounds to 0.53?

- ⃝ 0.514
- ⃝ 0.537
- ⃝ 0.541
- ⃝ 0.528

Word Form

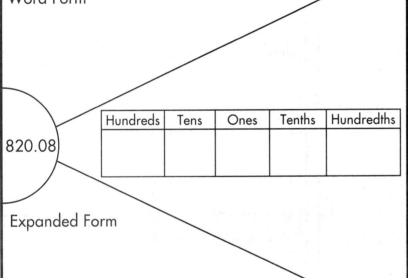

820.08

Hundreds	Tens	Ones	Tenths	Hundredths

Expanded Form

4 yards = _____ feet

Shade $\frac{1}{4}$.

Draw all lines of symmetry for the equilateral triangle.

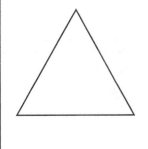

Place each fraction on the number line. Then, round to the nearest whole number.

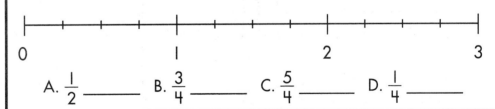

A. $\frac{1}{2}$ _____   B. $\frac{3}{4}$ _____   C. $\frac{5}{4}$ _____   D. $\frac{1}{4}$ _____

Write as a decimal.

nineteen hundredths

$\frac{1}{3} + \frac{2}{3} =$ _____

Selma needs 48 ounces of chocolate chips for her cookie recipe. How many pounds of chocolate should she buy?

If a square has 7-inch sides, what is its perimeter? What is its area?

1 milliliter is 1,000 times less liquid than 1 _____.

A rectangular restaurant kitchen measures 9 meters long and 12 meters wide. What is the total area of the kitchen? Show your work.

Which phrase means
(65 ÷ 5) − 4?

○ divide 65 by 5, then add 4

○ divide 65 by 5, then subtract 4

○ divide 5 by 65, then subtract 4

○ add 4, then divide 65 by 5

0.300 ◯ 0.40

22,852
+   529
‾‾‾‾‾‾‾

7 cm

11 cm

Perimeter _____

Area _____

637 ÷ 7 =

On a coordinate plane, the x-axis and the y-axis intersect at a point. What is this point called? _____
Draw and label this point.

Name _____

Draw a pair of perpendicular lines.

How do you know they are perpendicular?

_____

_____

List the factors of 24. Circle the factors that are prime numbers.

$\frac{1}{4}$ ◯ $\frac{2}{3}$

Draw a parallelogram.

List the properties.
Sides:
Vertices:
Other:

+ 0.6

0.4 ⇨ ____
3.1 ⇨ ____
2.2 ⇨ ____
0.8 ⇨ ____
1.4 ⇨ ____
4.0 ⇨ ____
5.2 ⇨ ____
2.7 ⇨ ____

Rita's Garden

		X	
		X	X
X		X	X
X	X	X	X	X
$\frac{5}{6}$	$\frac{6}{6}$	$1\frac{1}{6}$	$1\frac{2}{6}$	$1\frac{3}{6}$

Height of Corn Plants (inches)

How many corn plants did Rita plant in her garden?

Write as a decimal.

five and sixteen thousandths

$4,000 \times 4 =$ ____

☆ $\times 6 = 18$

$18 \div 6 =$ ☆

Start: 2.6   **Subtract 8.3**   **Finish: ____**

Add 12.1   **Add 3.9**

Write an equation for the problem.

Pablo is six inches shorter than his older brother.

3,407
×   7

Round the answer to the nearest

ten thousand

_____

thousand

_____

hundred

_____

ten

_____

Sophie has been saving her money. Does she have enough money to buy a $30 building set?

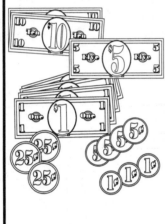

Write each as an expression.

The difference between nineteen and five, divided by two.

Add twenty-five and eight, then multiply by three.

67.98
+ 0.67

Fill in the missing number.

[   ]
− 4.4
  2.2

Which of the following is equal to $\frac{5}{100}$?

○ 5.0   ○ 0.5

○ 0.05   ○ 0.005

Rule: Divide by 10

10,000, _____, _____, _____, _____

Identify the coordinate pair for each point on the graph.

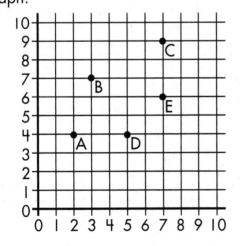

A _____   B _____   C _____

D _____   E _____

---

15 feet = _____ yards

_____ feet = 7 yards

30 feet = _____ yards

Name _____   **Week 4, Day 3**

Compare using **>**, **<**, or **=**.

0.52 ◯ 0.2

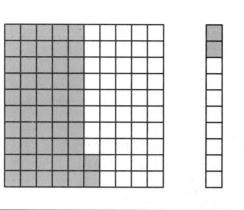

Which decimal rounds to 6?

◯ 6.535

◯ 5.369

◯ 5.672

◯ 5.006

Word Form

704.04

Expanded Form

Hundreds	Tens	Ones	Tenths	Hundredths

4 yards ◯ 12 feet

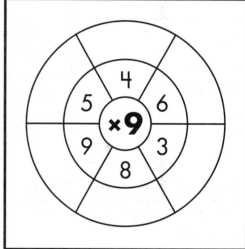

$\frac{3}{8}$ is closest to which benchmark number?

Color your answer.

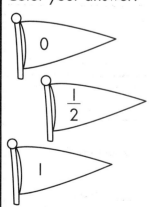

Six friends want to share two cookies. How much will each friend get? Show your work.

18.453
Round to the nearest

hundredth _____

tenth _____

whole number _____

$\frac{1}{12}$ ◯ $\frac{1}{10}$

What is the expanded form for 15.38?

○ $(1 \times 10) + (5 \times 1) + (3 \times \frac{1}{100}) + (8 \times \frac{1}{1,000})$

○ $(1 \times 10) + (5 \times 1) + (3 \times \frac{1}{10}) + (8 \times \frac{1}{100})$

○ $(1 \times 10) + (5 \times 1) + (3 \times \frac{1}{10}) + (8 \times \frac{1}{1,000})$

○ $(1 \times 100) + (5 \times 10) + (3 \times \frac{1}{100}) + (8 \times \frac{1}{1,000})$

Which operation should you perform first to solve $2 \times [(2 + 5) - 5]$?

○ division   ○ multiplication

○ addition   ○ subtraction

Write an expression.
n decreased by 21

The groundskeeper mowed $\frac{3}{8}$ of the field before he ran out of gas. How much more does he have left to mow?

Write the decimal for the shaded part.

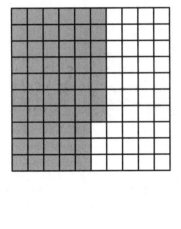

_____

0.999 ◯ 1.01

Round 546.279 to the nearest whole number.

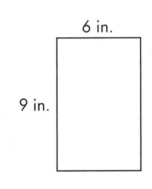

6 in.

9 in.

Perimeter _____

Area _____

List the factors of 36.

Write a mixed number to represent the shaded area. _____

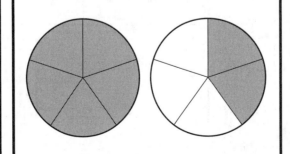

Draw a dotted line to represent the line of symmetry in this figure.

Fill in the missing number.

$$\begin{array}{r} \boxed{} \\ -\ 2.03 \\ \hline 3.99 \end{array}$$

3, 12, 21, 30, 39, . . .

Rule _____

What is the name of the angle that measures between 0° and 90°?

Draw an example.

Round each number to the place of the underlined digit.

3<u>4</u>5.45 _____

4,670.5<u>2</u> _____

2<u>8</u>3.5 _____

892.<u>3</u>3 _____

10<u>5</u>.67 _____

Plot the points on the coordinate plane.

A (1, 3)   **B** (3, 2)   **C** (4, 4)
  D (2, 5)   **E** (0, 0)

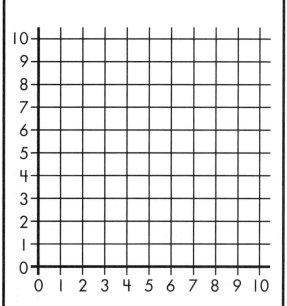

Write 291.32 in word form.

72 × 100 = _____

9 × 2 = ✧

18 ÷ 2 = ✧

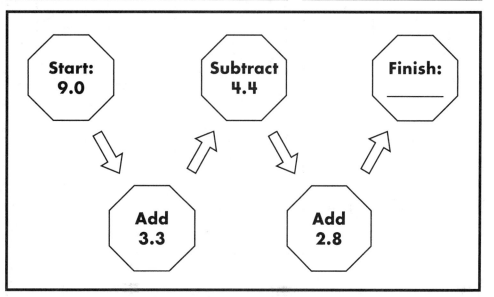

Start: 9.0   Subtract 4.4   Finish: _____

Add 3.3   Add 2.8

Which of the following would round to 15.75?

○ 15.7 ○ 15.746

○ 15.755 ○ 15.756

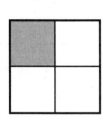

Write the shaded part as a decimal and a fraction.

fraction _____

decimal _____

What time will it be in $2\frac{1}{4}$ hours?

_____

Solve. What patterns do you see?

6 × 7 = _____	12 × 3 = _____
60 × 7 = _____	120 × 3 = _____
600 × 7 = _____	1,200 × 3 = _____
8 × 4 = _____	9 × 2 = _____
80 × 4 = _____	90 × 2 = _____
800 × 4 = _____	900 × 2 = _____

787.5
+ 532.89

What is the value of the 4 in 24,307?

Which two fractions are equivalent?

○ $\frac{1}{2}$ and $\frac{6}{10}$ ○ $\frac{2}{3}$ and $\frac{4}{6}$

○ $\frac{2}{3}$ and $\frac{3}{2}$ ○ $\frac{1}{4}$ and $\frac{3}{4}$

Rule: Add 4

2, _____, _____, _____, _____

Evaluate the numerical expression.

21 ÷ (10 – 3)

Plot the points on the coordinate plane.

M (1, 1)   **A** (2, 2)
T (3, 3)   **H** (4, 4)

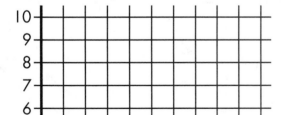

Shade to represent 1.3.

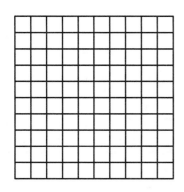

Katrina ran the 100-yard dash in 21.014 seconds. Which of the following expresses this time in words?

○ twenty-one and fourteen hundredths

○ twenty-one and fourteen tenths

○ twenty-one and fourteen thousandths

○ twenty-one thousand fourteen

Word Form

Expanded Form

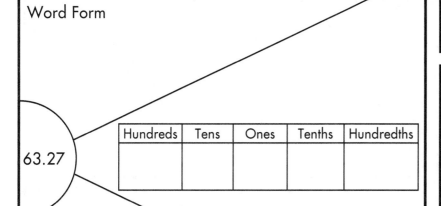

Hundreds	Tens	Ones	Tenths	Hundredths

63.27

3 meters = _____ millimeters

Shade $\frac{3}{4}$.

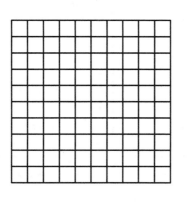

Circle the greater number without multiplying.

99

or

99 × $\frac{1}{5}$

Place each fraction on the number line. Then, round to the nearest whole number.

0   1   2

A. $\frac{1}{3}$ _____   B. $\frac{6}{3}$ _____   C. $\frac{4}{3}$ _____   D. $\frac{2}{3}$ _____

Write as a decimal.

$$(5 \times \frac{1}{10}) + (3 \times \frac{1}{100})$$

$\frac{4}{10}$ ◯ $\frac{2}{3}$

What is the expanded form for 78.16?

○ $(7 \times 10) + (8 \times 1) + (1 \times 1/\frac{1}{100}) + (6 \times \frac{1}{1,000})$

○ $(7 \times 10) + (8 \times 1) + (1 \times \frac{1}{10}) + (1 \times \frac{1}{100})$

○ $(7 \times 10) + (8 \times 1) + (1 \times \frac{1}{10}) + (6 \times \frac{1}{100})$

○ $(7 \times 100) + (8 \times 10) + (1 \times \frac{1}{100}) + (6 \times \frac{1}{1,000})$

Which operation should you perform first to solve $14 + (2 \times 5) - 2$?

○ division   ○ multiplication

○ addition   ○ subtraction

I quart is _____ times more liquid than I pint.

Javon measured the diameters of several flowers.

What is the difference between the sizes of the two largest flowers? _____
What is the difference between the sizes of the largest and the smallest flowers? _____
Would the daisy and the hibiscus equal the sunflower in size? _____

Hibiscus	4.4 in.
Peony	5.75 in.
Daisy	3.12 in.
Sunflower	9.25 in.

Write the decimal for the shaded part.

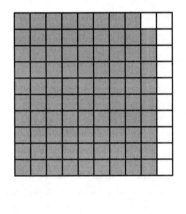

_____

0.55 ◯ 0.542

777
− 382

5 ft.

15 ft.

Perimeter _____

Area _____

List the factors of 42.

KJ bought three candy bars at the store for $1.29 each. How much did he spend?

Name _____

What is the value of p? _____

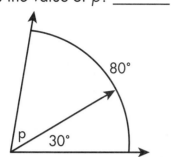

53.88
+ 85.98

$\frac{1}{8}$ ◯ $\frac{1}{4}$

Name and draw a quadrilateral that has no right angles.

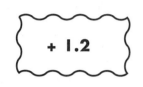

0.6 ⟹ _____

2.1 ⟹ _____

2.9 ⟹ _____

0.7 ⟹ _____

5.3 ⟹ _____

2.8 ⟹ _____

6.2 ⟹ _____

3.4 ⟹ _____

Alyssa walked her dog each day last week. The line plot shows how far she walked each day.

X		X	X
X	X	X	X
$\frac{1}{2}$	1	$1\frac{1}{2}$	2

Daily Walks (miles)

How many miles did she walk last week?

Write as a decimal.

four and nineteen thousandths

1,000 × 98 = _____

---

3 × ✦ = 27

27 ÷ 9 = ✦

Color the circles that are greater than 0.45

(0.5)   (0.29)   (0.46)   (0.3)   (0.7)

(0.4)   (0.09)   (0.9)   (0.29)   (0.42)

(0.6)   (0.40)   (0.62)   (0.12)   (0.49)

What is the remainder when 1,027 is divided by 10?

○ 7   ○ 2   ○ 5   ○ 4

Which expression does not have a value of 5?

○ 2 + (7 × 2) − 11

○ (8 ÷ 4) + (1 + 2)

○ 4 + 6 ÷ 2 − 2

○ 2 × (6 − 2) ÷ 2

6,035
×   8

Round the answer to the nearest

ten thousand

_____

thousand

_____

hundred

_____

ten

_____

Kevin

Tommy

Who won the race? Explain how you know.

365.54
− 26.23

Fill in the missing number.

− 3.8
1.7

Which two fractions are equivalent?

○ $\frac{6}{7}$ and $\frac{7}{8}$ ○ $\frac{1}{3}$ and $\frac{3}{1}$

○ $\frac{4}{16}$ and $\frac{1}{4}$ ○ $\frac{4}{5}$ and $\frac{9}{10}$

Rule: Multiply by 10

12, _____, _____, _____, _____

Write 4.93 in expanded form.

Plot the points on the coordinate plane.

A (0, 2)   **B** (2, 4)
C (4, 4)   **D** (6, 2)

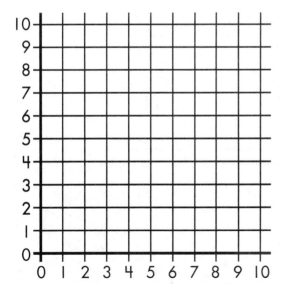

Compare using **>**, **<**, or **=**.

0.7 ◯ 0.49

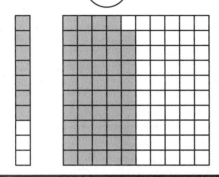

Which decimal represents

$4 \times 100 + 1 \times 10 + 6 \times 1 + 3 \times \dfrac{1}{10} + 5 \times \dfrac{1}{1000}$?

◯ 416.350

◯ 406.305

◯ 416.035

◯ 416.305

Word Form

42.789

Tens	Ones	Tenths	Hundredths	Thousandths

Expanded Form

540 sec. ◯ 8 min.

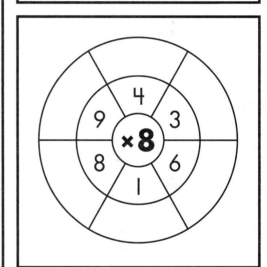

$\dfrac{2}{5}$ is closer to which benchmark number?

Color your answer.

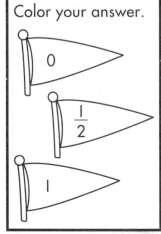

0

$\dfrac{1}{2}$

1

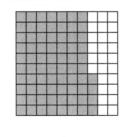 ◯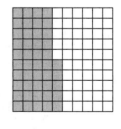

_____   _____

27.211

Round to the nearest

hundredth _____

tenth _____

whole number _____

$\dfrac{2}{5}$ ◯ $\dfrac{1}{10}$

Which of the following is equal to five hundred five thousand and twenty-nine thousandths?

○ 505.29   ○ 505,000.29

○ 505,000.029   ○ 505,029

Circle the largest number. Underline the smallest number.

44.54, 45.44, 54.32, 54.48, 44.99

Write an expression.
9 increased by x

Janet and Don walked $\frac{1}{4}$ of a mile on Tuesday, $\frac{1}{2}$ of a mile on Wednesday, and $\frac{3}{4}$ of a mile on Thursday. How much did they walk altogether?

Write the decimal for the shaded part.

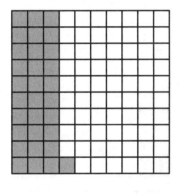

_____

5.128 ◯ 5.136

345.87
− 101.88

Kilometers	Meters
1	
	3,000
5	
	7,000
	12,000

Estimate the product.
66 × 5

How many minutes are in $\frac{2}{3}$ of an hour? How do you know?

Look at the figure below. Draw how it would look if you rotated the figure 270° clockwise.

Write a fraction describing nine birds in two nests. If possible, reduce the fraction to lowest terms.

0, 15, 30, 45, 60, ...

Rule _____

Draw and label the quadrilateral that has four congruent sides and no right angles.

Round each number to the place of the underlined digit.

767.1 _____

400.27 _____

963.26 _____

34.841 _____

28.388 _____

The teacher asked her class how many books they read over spring break. Use the data below to create a line plot.

2, 0, 1, 3, 3, 0, 4, 1, 4, 0, 2, 3, 1, 4, 2, 2, 1, 0, 4, 2

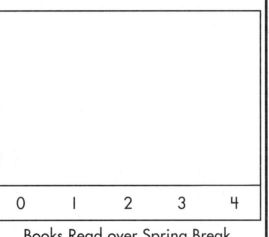

Books Read over Spring Break

What is the word form of 1,042.38?

487.49 × 10

= _____

7 × ⭐ = 21

21 ÷ 3 = ⭐

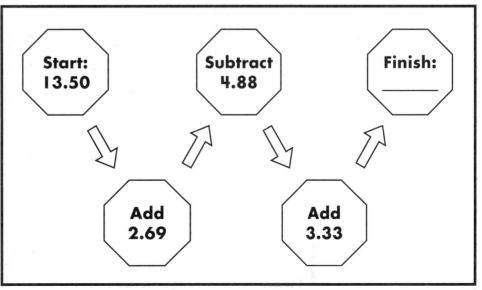

Which of the following would round to 9?

◯ 8.48   ◯ 8.9

◯ 8.09   ◯ 8.348

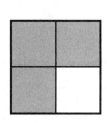

Write the shaded part as a decimal and a fraction.

fraction _____

decimal _____

What time will it be in $3\frac{3}{4}$ hours?

_____

Solve. What patterns do you see?

36 ÷ 3 = _____	42 ÷ 6 = _____
360 ÷ 3 = _____	420 ÷ 6 = _____
3,600 ÷ 3 = _____	4,200 ÷ 6 = _____
32 ÷ 8 = _____	18 ÷ 2 = _____
320 ÷ 8 = _____	180 ÷ 2 = _____
3,200 ÷ 8 = _____	1,800 ÷ 2 = _____

45.38
– 3.26

What is the value of the 1 in 234,793.1?

Which two fractions are equivalent?

◯ $\frac{9}{10}$ and $\frac{18}{20}$ ◯ $\frac{5}{15}$ and $\frac{1}{4}$

◯ $\frac{4}{5}$ and $\frac{6}{7}$ ◯ $\frac{1}{2}$ and $\frac{19}{30}$

Rule: Add 6

3, _____, _____, _____, _____

Evaluate the numerical expression.

8 + 18 ÷ 2

Identify the points on the graph.

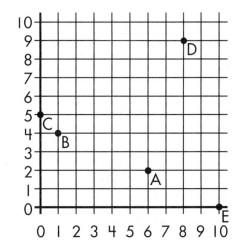

A _____   B _____   C _____

D _____   E _____

Shade to represent 1.08.

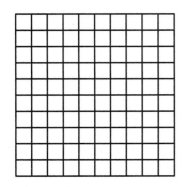

Most adults have 206 bones in their body. How many bones do 11 adults have altogether?

○ 612

○ 2,266

○ 412

○ 2,206

Word Form

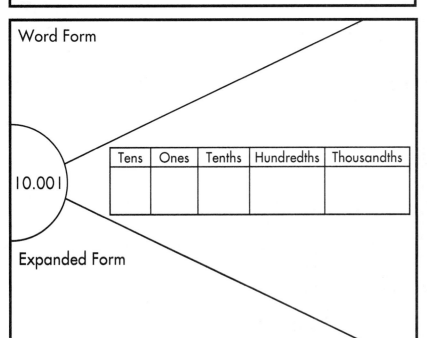

10.001

Tens	Ones	Tenths	Hundredths	Thousandths

Expanded Form

1,000 g = _____ kg

Use the geoboard to show $\frac{1}{4} + \frac{1}{2}$.

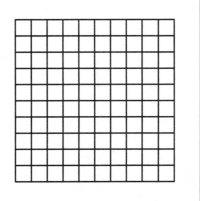

Circle the greater number without multiplying.

$551 \times \frac{1}{8}$

or

551

Place each fraction on the number line. Then, round to the nearest whole number.

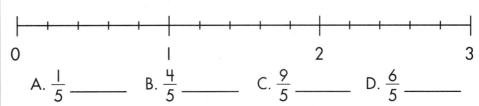

0   1   2   3

A. $\frac{1}{5}$ _____   B. $\frac{4}{5}$ _____   C. $\frac{9}{5}$ _____   D. $\frac{6}{5}$ _____

Write as a decimal.

$(7 \times \frac{1}{10}) + (3 \times \frac{1}{100}) + (9 \times \frac{1}{1000})$

$\frac{3}{4}$ ○ $\frac{3}{7}$

What is the expanded form for 93.04?

○ $(9 \times 100) + (3 \times 1) + (4 \times \frac{1}{1,000})$

○ $(9 \times 10) + (3 \times 1) + (4 \times \frac{1}{10})$

○ $(9 \times 10) + (3 \times 1) + (4 \times \frac{1}{100})$

○ $(9 \times 10) + (3 \times 10) + (4 \times \frac{1}{1,000})$

Which operation should you perform first to solve $[8 \times (5 - 2)] \div 2$?

○ division   ○ multiplication

○ addition   ○ subtraction

---

1 meter is 1,000 times shorter than 1 _____.

Parker and Travon hope to catch a 5-pound fish. Parker keeps throwing the fish back because they don't weigh 5 pounds. Travon thinks they could keep some by rounding the weights to the nearest whole number. Circle the fish that round to 5 pounds.

Write the decimal for the shaded part.

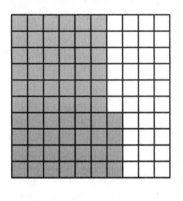

_____

73.15 ◯ 73.25

7,000
- 688

---

9 ft.

16 ft.

Perimeter _____

Area _____

Estimate the product.

48×4

Jose's class ate $2\frac{1}{4}$ pizzas. Carl's class ate $2\frac{3}{4}$ pizzas. How much pizza did both classes eat?

What is the area of the figure below?

3 ft.

4 ft.

Fill in the missing number.

$$+\ 3.81 \over 9.00$$

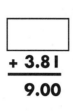

Name two quadrilaterals that have four right angles. Draw them.

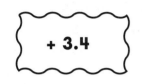

+ 3.4

0.4 ⟹ _____

2.2 ⟹ _____

1.8 ⟹ _____

7.6 ⟹ _____

0.3 ⟹ _____

6.0 ⟹ _____

4.9 ⟹ _____

2.7 ⟹ _____

Use the data to complete the line plot.

19, $19\frac{1}{2}$, 20, 18, 18, 19, 20, 18,

$19\frac{1}{2}$, 18

18	$18\frac{1}{2}$	___	$19\frac{1}{2}$	20

Shoestring Length

Write as a decimal.

eight and twenty-seven hundredths

$39.52 \times 10 =$ _____

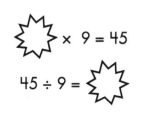 × 9 = 45

45 ÷ 9 =

Color the circles that are less than or equal to 0.2.

 0.11   0.3   0.09   0.8   0.19

0.22   0.20   0.01   0.1   0.21

0.6   0.40   0.13   0.5   0.39

45

How many hundredths are equivalent to 8 tenths?

○ 800   ○ 8

○ 70   ○ 80

Rule: +1	Rule: + 3	Ordered Pair
0	0	(0, 0)
1	3	(1, 3)

8,371
× 9

Round the answer to the nearest

ten thousand

_____

thousand

_____

hundred

_____

ten

_____

A monthly membership to the community gym is $35. In January, the gym had 872 members. How much money did the gym get for memberships in January? Show your work.

3,478.24
- 356.37

$2 + 5 \times (1 + 2) =$

Round 5,577.089 to each place.

hundredths _____
tenths   _____
ones   _____
tens   _____
hundreds   _____
thousands   _____

Rule: Divide by 10

500,000, _____, _____, _____

Write 38.28 in word form.

Fill in the missing numbers. Add two numbers beside each other to get the number above them.

1.3

0.5   0.8   0.4   0.7   0.6

Compare using **>**, **<**, or **=**.

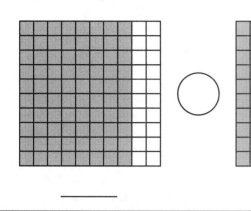

_____   _____

Humans have about 650 muscles. How many muscles would 20 adult humans have?

○ 1,300

○ 130,000

○ 670

○ 13,000

Word Form

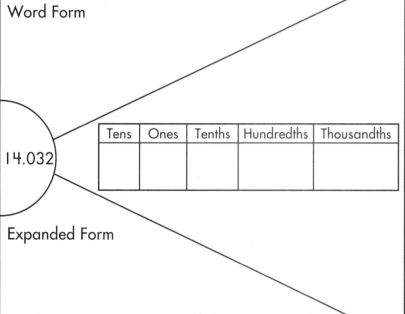

14.032

Tens	Ones	Tenths	Hundredths	Thousandths

Expanded Form

2,250 lb. ○ 1 T

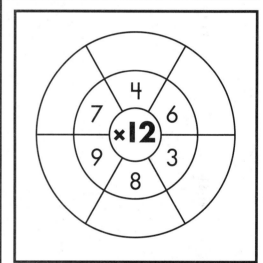

$\frac{6}{7}$ is closer to which benchmark number? Color your answer.

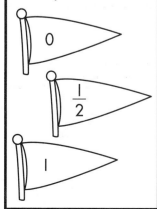

0

$\frac{1}{2}$

1

Becca works on her reading homework for $\frac{1}{2}$ hour and on her math homework for $\frac{1}{4}$ hour. How much time does Becca spend on homework? Use the number line to help find the answer.

0   1

347.946
Round to the nearest

hundredth _____

tenth _____

whole number _____

$\frac{3}{4}$ ○ $\frac{4}{10}$

Name _____   **Week 8, Day 4**

Circle the largest number. Underline the smallest number.

709.8, 709.9, 709.799, 709.700, 709.82

Put the measurements in order from least to greatest.

5 cm, 5 km, 5 m, 5 mm

_____, _____, _____, _____

Write an expression.
x reduced by 33

Ayako used $1\frac{1}{3}$ cups nuts, $\frac{2}{3}$ cup raisins, and $\frac{1}{3}$ cup chocolate chips to make trail mix. How many cups of trail mix did she make in all?

Write the decimal for the shaded part.

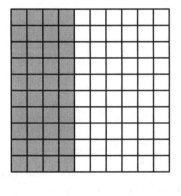

_____

82.003 ◯ 82.03

890.05
− 432.71
‾‾‾‾‾‾‾

Milligrams	Grams
2,000	
	5
9,000	
	10
15,000	

Estimate the product.
72 × 7

A large crate holds 16 boxes. Each box has 12 smaller boxes of candy bars inside. How many candy bars are in each crate?

Name _____

What is the perimeter of the figure?

6 in.

6 in.

Write a fraction to show 8 sandwiches shared by 12 people. If possible, reduce the fraction to lowest terms.

0, 12, 24, 36, 48, . . .

Rule _____

Which figure is an equilateral triangle?

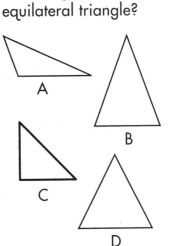

A

B

C

D

+ 2.6

4.1 ⟹ ____

2.2 ⟹ ____

1.5 ⟹ ____

6.2 ⟹ ____

0.4 ⟹ ____

2.7 ⟹ ____

3.2 ⟹ ____

1.6 ⟹ ____

Using the line plot below, find the total weight of pumpkins weighing less than 11 pounds.

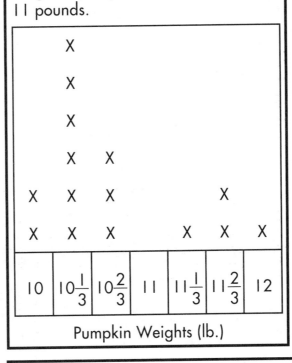

Pumpkin Weights (lb.)

What is the word form of 102.03?

100×314.78

= _____

$8 \times$ ⭐ $= 72$

⭐ $\div 8 = 9$

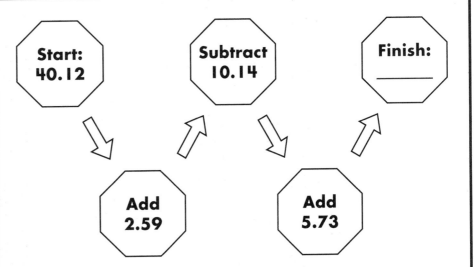

Start: 40.12

Subtract 10.14

Finish: ____

Add 2.59

Add 5.73

Round 13.462 to the nearest tenth.

○ 13.05   ○ 13.4

○ 13.5   ○ 13.46

Solve. What patterns do you see?

9 × 3 = _____	8 × 9 = _____
90 × 3 = _____	80 × 9 = _____
900 × 3 = _____	800 × 9 = _____
12 × 4 = _____	6 × 4 = _____
120 × 4 = _____	60 × 4 = _____
1,200 × 4 = _____	600 × 4 = _____

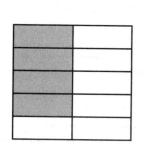

Write the shaded part as a decimal and a fraction.

fraction _____

decimal _____

What time will it be in $3\frac{1}{2}$ hours?

_____

389.31
−   0.46

What is the value of the 9 in 0.092?

Which two fractions are equivalent?

○ $\frac{50}{100}$ and $\frac{5}{25}$ ○ $\frac{18}{27}$ and $\frac{2}{3}$

○ $\frac{99}{100}$ and $\frac{9}{10}$ ○ $\frac{3}{2}$ and $\frac{4}{3}$

Rule: Subtract 4

36, _____, _____, _____, _____

Evaluate the numerical expression.

(99 ÷ 9) × 4

Kade wanted to map his town square. Draw the following objects where they belong.

Water fountain (3, 3)   Statue (7, 7)

Bench (7, 3)   Oak tree (3, 7)

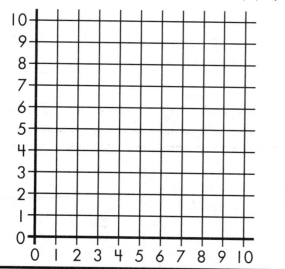

Shade to represent 1.7

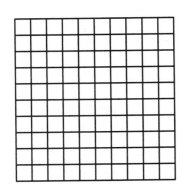

65.33 + 4.18 = {   }

○ 69.41

○ 69.51

○ 70.51

○ 61.15

Word Form

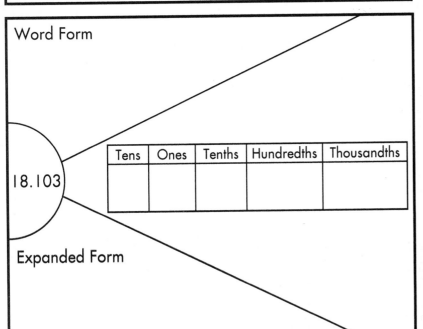

Tens	Ones	Tenths	Hundredths	Thousandths

18.103

Expanded Form

3 L = _____ mL

Shade $\frac{6}{8}$.

Circle the greater number without multiplying.

67 × 84

or

84

Place each mixed number on the number line. Then, round to the nearest whole number.

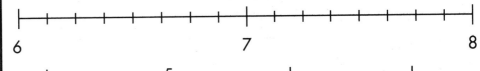

6   7   8

A. $6\frac{1}{4}$ _____   B. $7\frac{5}{8}$ _____   C. $7\frac{1}{2}$ _____   D. $7\frac{1}{8}$ _____

Write as a decimal.

$(4 \times 1) + (5 \times \frac{1}{100}) + (9 \times \frac{1}{1,000})$

$\frac{5}{6}$ ○ $\frac{2}{3}$

What is the expanded form for 61.024?

○ $(6 \times 10) + (1 \times 1) + (2 \times \frac{1}{10}) + (4 \times \frac{1}{1,000})$

○ $(6 \times 100) + (1 \times 1) + (2 \times \frac{1}{100}) + (4 \times \frac{1}{1,000})$

○ $(6 \times 10) + (1 \times 1) + (2 \times \frac{1}{100}) + (4 \times \frac{1}{1,000})$

○ $(6 \times 10) + (1 \times 1) + (2 \times \frac{1}{10}) + (4 \times \frac{1}{100})$

Which operation should you perform first so solve $3 + [4 \times (9 - 6)]$?

○ division   ○ multiplication

○ addition   ○ subtraction

---

1 _____ is 12 times as long as 1 inch.

Rob decided to double his cookie recipe since his friends were coming over. The original recipe called for $\frac{2}{3}$ cup of chocolate chips. How many total chocolate chips does Rob need now since he doubled the recipe?

Write the decimal for the shaded part.

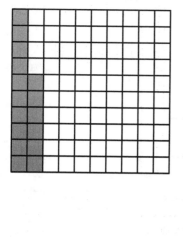

_____

7.645 ◯ 7.654

32,950
− 6,977

---

9 ft.

20 ft.

Perimeter _____

Area _____

Estimate the product.

91 × 5

Paco ordered 15 dozen donuts. How many donuts did Paco order in all?

Name _____

What time will it be in two and a half hours? _____

Fill in the missing number.

$$\begin{array}{r} \boxed{} \\ -\ 8.39 \\ \hline 1.03 \end{array}$$

$\dfrac{6}{8}$ ◯ $\dfrac{3}{4}$

Write all the names this quadrilateral could be called.

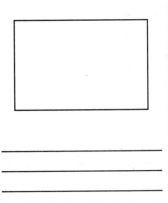

_____
_____
_____

+ 3.1

0.4 ⟹ _____

2.4 ⟹ _____

1.6 ⟹ _____

2.3 ⟹ _____

1.4 ⟹ _____

0.5 ⟹ _____

3.4 ⟹ _____

5.9 ⟹ _____

250 ÷ 10 = _____

$12 \times$ ✦ $= 48$

$48 \div 12 =$ ✦

The teacher asked students how many pencils they had at their desks. Use the data below to create the line plot.

2, 0, 1, 3, 3, 0, 4, 1, 4, 0, 2, 3, 1, 4, 2, 2, 1, 0, 4, 2

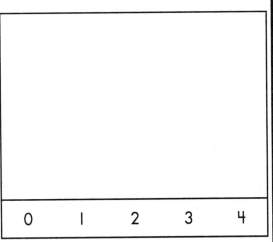

| 0 | 1 | 2 | 3 | 4 |

Books Read Over Spring Break

Write as a decimal.

thirteen hundredths

Color the circles that are greater than 0.4.

 0.39   0.6   0.298   0.5   0.040

0.200   0.8   0.42   0.7   0.40

0.30   0.900   0.009   0.41   0.099

How many thousandths are equivalent to 50 hundredths?

○ 50   ○ 500

○ 5   ○ 5,000

The car salesman has a sale on 4 identical trucks. Each truck costs $14,879. If the salesman sold all 4 trucks in one week, how much money did he make?
Show your work.

Rule: +2	Rule: +4	Ordered Pair
0	0	(0, 0)
2	4	(2, 4)

Evelyn hit her golf ball 124 yards. She then hit her ball 16 feet to the green. For her last shot, she hit the ball 28 inches. How many inches did Evelyn hit the ball altogether?

56.89
− 45.46

$\dfrac{1}{4}$

$+ \dfrac{3}{6}$

Myong is collecting rainwater for the garden. In the first week, she collected 5 gallons. In the second week, she collected 12 quarts. In week three, she collected 7 pints. How many cups of water did she collect in all? Make a table to help sort your information.

90.11 × 13.24 = ⟨_____⟩

○ 76.36

○ 75.87

○ 76.87

○ 83.33

Rule: Multiply by 10

3.2, _____, _____, _____, _____

Write 873.17 in expanded form.

Compare using **>**, **<**, or **=**.

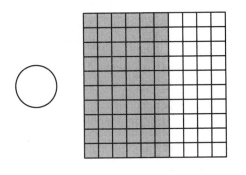

_____   _____

72.03 – 18.58

- ◯ 53.45
- ◯ 66.55
- ◯ 53.55
- ◯ 54.45

Word Form

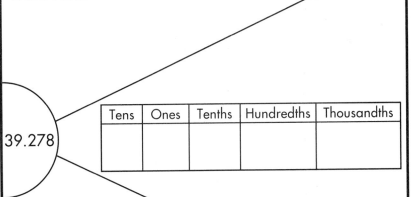

Tens	Ones	Tenths	Hundredths	Thousandths

39.278

Expanded Form

---

6 kg ◯ 600 g

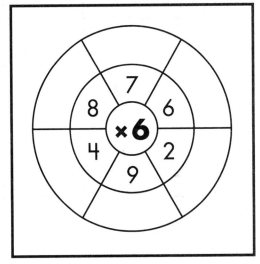

$4\overline{)2{,}856}$

Circle the point on the number line that represents $2\frac{6}{10}$.

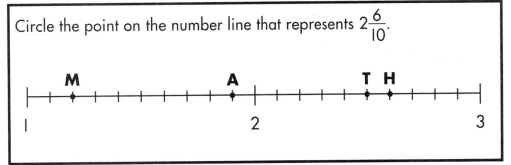

55.736

Round to the nearest

hundredth _____

tenth _____

whole number _____

$\frac{4}{20}$ ◯ $\frac{8}{16}$

Which of the following is equal to four hundred sixty-eight and nineteen hundredths?

○ 468.019   ○ 468.19

○ 460.819   ○ 400.68

Put the measurements in order from least to greatest.

4 yd., 4 in., 4 mi., 4 ft.

_____, _____, _____, _____

Write an expression.
c fewer than 126

Mark spent $\frac{1}{3}$ of an hour on his homework as soon as he got home. After band practice, he worked on his homework again for $\frac{1}{2}$ an hour. How much time did Mark spend on his homework?

Kelsey said that $11 \times 5 + 3$ equals 3. Luke said the answer is 9. How did they each work the problem to come up with a different answer? Show your work.

Kelsey
Luke

0.866 ◯ 0.688

$5 + (2 \times 13) =$

Liters	Milliliters
	3,000
7	
	9,000
5	
	6,000

14
– 11

Solve.

$78.41 \times 10^1 = $ _____

$78.41 \times 10^2 = $ _____

$78.41 \times 10^3 = $ _____

$78.41 \times 10^4 = $ _____

Shade the model to represent $4 \times \frac{1}{3}$.

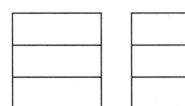

$98\overline{)1960}$

3, 7, 11, 15, 19, . . .

Rule _____

Which figure is an isosceles triangle?

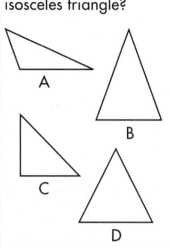

Round each number to the place of the underlined digit.

546.0<u>8</u> _____

9,820.0<u>4</u>9 _____

4<u>8</u>9.67 _____

1,002.9<u>9</u> _____

20<u>9</u>.33 _____

Plot the points on the coordinate plane.

(0, 1), (5, 1), (7, 6), (2, 6)

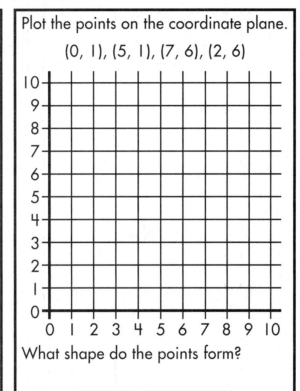

What shape do the points form?

_____

Write 607.10 in word form.

4,500 ÷ 100

= _____

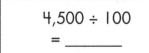
$\times 6 = 24$

$24 \div 4 =$

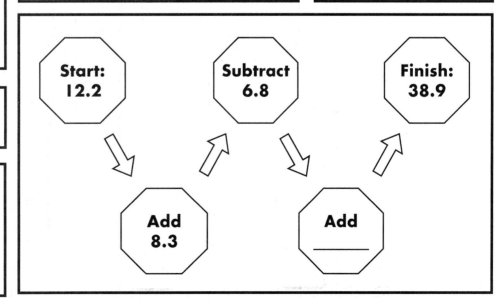

Start: 12.2

Add 8.3

Subtract 6.8

Add _____

Finish: 38.9

Round 4.938 to the nearest hundredth.

○ 5.0   ○ 4.94

○ 4.93   ○ 4.9

Solve. What patterns do you see?

27 ÷ 9 = _____	72 ÷ 8 = _____
270 ÷ 9 = _____	720 ÷ 8 = _____
2,700 ÷ 9 = _____	7,200 ÷ 8 = _____
48 ÷ 4 = _____	24 ÷ 6 = _____
480 ÷ 4 = _____	240 ÷ 6 = _____
4,800 ÷ 4 = _____	2,400 ÷ 6 = _____

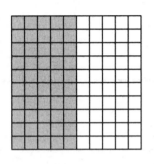

Write the shaded part as a decimal and a fraction.

fraction _____

decimal _____

What time will it be in $4\frac{3}{4}$ hours?

_____

560.3
– 34.04

What is the value of the 7 in 236.789?

347.816 + 29.48 = ⟨_____⟩

○ 350.764

○ 377.296

○ 366.296

○ 376.276

Rule: Subtract 7

84, _____, _____, _____, _____

Evaluate the numerical expression.

$$8 \times (4 + 1) \times 22$$

After the museum, Tyrell wants to visit the gift shop. Describe one path Tyrell could take to get to the gift shop.

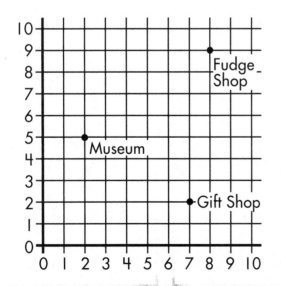

Name _____

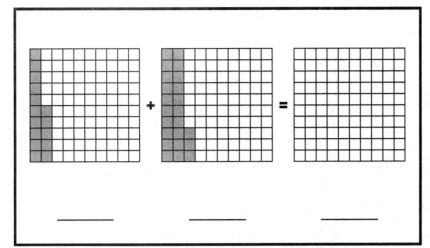

_____ + _____ = _____

Choose the measurement that is not equal to the others.

- ◯ 1 gal.
- ◯ 4 qt.
- ◯ 12 c.
- ◯ 64 fl. oz.

Word Form

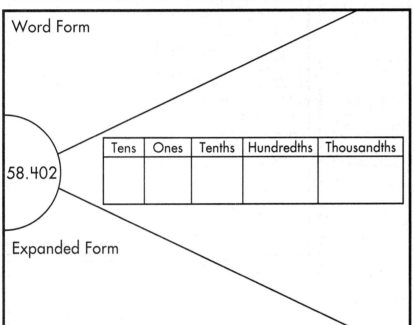

Tens	Ones	Tenths	Hundredths	Thousandths

58.402

Expanded Form

32 ounces = _____ pounds

Shade 0.25.

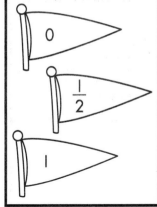

$\frac{10}{12}$ is closer to which benchmark number?

Color your answer.

0

$\frac{1}{2}$

1

Place each number on the number line. Then, round to the nearest whole number.

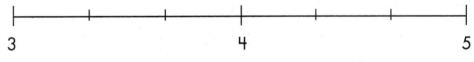

3   4   5

A. $4\frac{2}{3}$ _____   B. $3\frac{8}{12}$ _____   C. $3\frac{1}{3}$ _____   D. $4\frac{1}{3}$ _____

Write as a decimal.

four and fourteen thousandths

$\frac{1}{2}$ ◯ $\frac{17}{30}$

59

What decimal represents

$(7 \times 100) + (8 \times 10) + (7 \times \frac{1}{10}) + (3 \times \frac{1}{100})$?

○ 78.73   ○ 708.730

○ 780.73   ○ 780.073

Which decimal rounds to 6?

○ 6.863   ○ 6.421

○ 5.402   ○ 6.580

I _____ is 100 times shorter than 1 meter.

Marie needs $7\frac{3}{4}$ feet of ribbon to complete her craft project. She has one roll of striped ribbon with $3\frac{1}{2}$ feet left on it and one roll of solid ribbon with $4\frac{1}{2}$ feet. Does Marie have enough ribbon to complete her craft? Explain your answer.

Write the decimal for the shaded part.

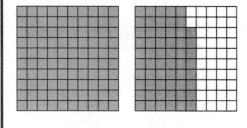

_____

1.64 ○ 1.640

892.1
+ 67.83

---

15 ft.

30 ft.

Perimeter _____

Area _____

1,285
×   6

Jada can walk 3 kilometers in one hour. How long does it her to walk 18 kilometers?

Name _____ **Week 12, Day 1**

Shade the model to represent $3 \times \dfrac{2}{5}$.

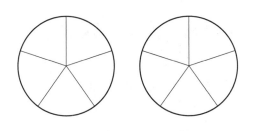

$$\begin{array}{r} \dfrac{1}{6} \\[6pt] +\ \dfrac{2}{3} \\ \hline \end{array}$$

$\dfrac{5}{6}$ ◯ $\dfrac{1}{2}$

Name three shapes that are quadrilaterals. Explain your reasoning.

+ 0.9

0.4 ⟹ _____

2.5 ⟹ _____

7.2 ⟹ _____

2.8 ⟹ _____

1.6 ⟹ _____

5.1 ⟹ _____

6.9 ⟹ _____

8.0 ⟹ _____

Color the path of equivalence from start to finish without diagonal movement.

Start: $\dfrac{1}{2}$	$\dfrac{2}{3}$	$\dfrac{12}{15}$
$\dfrac{6}{12}$	$\dfrac{2}{4}$	$\dfrac{5}{8}$
$\dfrac{1}{3}$	$\dfrac{10}{20}$	$\dfrac{1}{6}$
$\dfrac{8}{9}$	$\dfrac{30}{60}$	$\dfrac{7}{14}$
$\dfrac{4}{6}$	$\dfrac{2}{8}$	Finish!

Write as a decimal.

seventy-two and three tenths

$36.45 \div 10 = $ _____

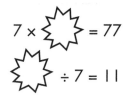

$7 \times \boxed{} = 77$

$\boxed{} \div 7 = 11$

Color the circles that are less than or equal to 0.67.

(0.9) (0.60) (0.8) (0.400) (0.321)

(0.670) (0.609) (0.008) (0.77) (0.68)

(0.099) (0.69) (0.6) (0.700) (0.09)

How many hundredths are equivalent to 2 tenths?

○ 2   ○ 200

○ 20   ○ 2,000

Rule: +1	Rule: +4	Ordered Pair
0	0	(0, 0)

6,677

×   4

Round the answer to the nearest

ten thousand

_____

thousand

_____

hundred

_____

ten

_____

Carlos has 1,248 baseball cards in his collection. Eight cards will fit on each page of the card album. How many pages does Carlos use if he organizes all of his cards in the album?

700.75

+   89.9

Fill in the missing number.

2.8

− [   ]

5.4

How many minutes are in one day?

_____

How many minutes are in one week?

_____

Rule: Divide by 10.

62,500, _____, _____, _____, _____

Write 5,681.04 in expanded form.

Fill in the missing numbers. Add two numbers beside each other to get the number above them.

8.02

5.64   2.38   1.74   6.71   9.04

Name _____ **Week 12, Day 3**

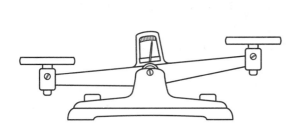

Write one of the measurements on each side to make the scale true.

    I kg   1,500 g

Diane bought 4 yards of fabric. She cut the fabric into 3 equal pieces. How long is each piece?

◯ 36 in.

◯ 48 in.

◯ 12 in.

◯ 16 in.

Word Form

43.862

Tens	Ones	Tenths	Hundredths	Thousandths

Expanded Form

2 L ◯ 2,500 mL

Which property of multiplication is shown?

(4 × 3) × 8 = 4 × (3 × 8)

◯ distributive

◯ identity

◯ associative

◯ commutative

7)6,349

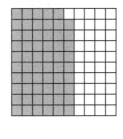 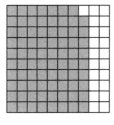

_____   _____

17.86
Round to the nearest

hundredth _____

tenth _____

whole number _____

$\frac{12}{18}$ ◯ $\frac{2}{3}$

© Carson-Dellosa • CD-104885   **63**

Circle the largest number. Underline the smallest number.

812.2, 811.897, 812.187, 812.15, 811.9

Put the measurements in order from least to greatest.

5 T., 5 oz., 5 lb.

_____, _____, _____

Write an expression.

174 less t

Barbara used $5\frac{1}{4}$ yards of fabric to make curtains. She had $2\frac{3}{8}$ yards left over. How much fabric did she have to begin with?

Write the decimal for the shaded part.

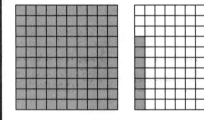

_____

0.08 ◯ 0.059

How many inches are there in $5\frac{1}{2}$ feet?

$$\begin{array}{r} 897 \\ \times\ \ 4 \\ \hline \end{array}$$

Drew bought 28 packs of baseball cards. Each pack contained 11 cards. How many baseball cards did Drew buy?

Grams	Kilograms
2,000	
	5
	7
	3
8,000	

How many inches are in $2\frac{1}{2}$ yards?
Show your work using the yardstick.

|1 2 3 4 5 6 7 8 9 10 11 12 13 14 15 16 17 18 19 20 21 22 23 24 25 26 27 28 29 30 31 32 33 34 35 36|

What is the value of the 2 in 5,632?

1, 4, 16, 64, 256, . . .

Rule _____

Which figure is an obtuse triangle?

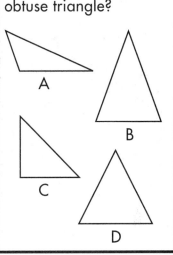

A

B

C

D

Round each number to the place of the underlined digit.

513.561 _____

187.25 _____

250.952 _____

900.96 _____

405.3 _____

Court purchased 2 notebooks for $1.20 each, 5 folders for $0.49 each, and one pack of pencils for $1.19. How much did Court spend on school supplies? Show your work.

Write 5.670 in word form.

$987.32 \div 10 =$ _____

$5 \times = 60$

$60 \div 5 =$

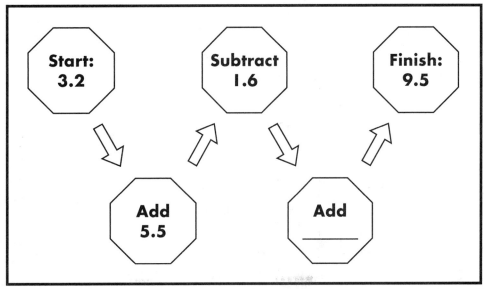

Start:
3.2

Subtract
1.6

Finish:
9.5

Add
5.5

Add
____

Write 1,179.363 in word form.

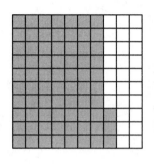

Write the shaded part as a decimal and a fraction.

fraction _____

decimal _____

5,580
× 6

Round the answer to the nearest

ten thousand

_____

thousand

_____

hundred

_____

ten

_____

Solve. What patterns do you see?

11 × 7 = _____	12 × 5 = _____
110 × 7 = _____	120 × 5 = _____
1,100 × 7 = _____	1,200 × 5 = _____
9 × 6 = _____	8 × 8 = _____
90 × 6 = _____	80 × 8 = _____
900 × 6 = _____	800 × 8 = _____

340
− 200.07

What is the value of the 6 in 100.67?

Kurt bought a 3-pack of footballs for $9.99. How much did each football cost?

Katrina stopped at the bank. She still needs to go to the grocery store before going home. How many more miles will Katrina travel before arriving home? Each unit is 1 mile. _____

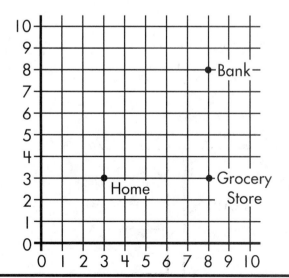

Rule: Subtract 6

42, _____, _____, _____, _____

Evaluate the numerical expression.

20 × 14 + (3 × 4)

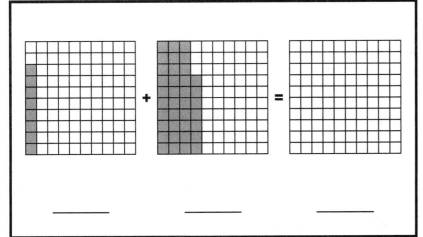

_____   _____   _____

A square belongs to all of the following groups except

◯ rectangles.

◯ trapezoids.

◯ quadrilaterals.

◯ parallelograms.

Word Form

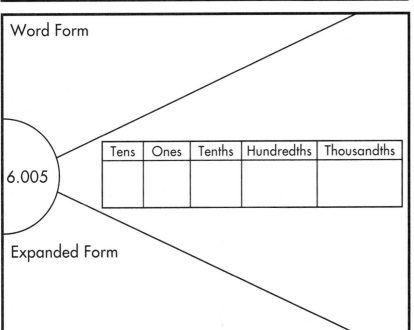

Tens	Ones	Tenths	Hundredths	Thousandths

6.005

Expanded Form

6 quarts = _____ cups

Use the geoboard to show $\frac{1}{4} + \frac{1}{8}$.

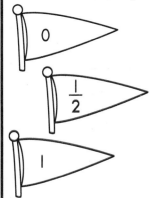

$\frac{1}{4}$ is closer to which benchmark number?

Color your answer.

0

$\frac{1}{2}$

1

Place each improper fraction on the number line. Then, round to the nearest whole number.

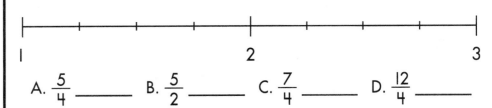

1   2   3

A. $\frac{5}{4}$ _____   B. $\frac{5}{2}$ _____   C. $\frac{7}{4}$ _____   D. $\frac{12}{4}$ _____

Write as a decimal.

$(4 \times 10) + (5 \times \frac{1}{10}) + (2 \times \frac{1}{1,000})$

$\frac{1}{4}$ ◯ $\frac{5}{16}$

Name _____

What decimal represents $(6 + 1,000) + (3 + 10)$ $+ (6 + \frac{1}{10}) + (3 + \frac{1}{1,000})$?

◯ 6,030.603   ◯ 6,030.063

◯ 630.63   ◯ 630.603

Which decimal rounds to 0.73?

◯ 0.711   ◯ 0.728

◯ 0.736   ◯ 0.703

1 _____ is 16 times as heavy as 1 ounce.

Adrianna painted $\frac{1}{4}$ of her room on Friday and $\frac{3}{8}$ of her room on Saturday. How much of her room has she painted so far?

Will needs 9 feet of ribbon for an art project. How many inches of ribbon should he buy if he's making four projects? Show your work.

473.394 ◯ 473.493

7,025
− 555

8 mi.

12 mi.

Perimeter _____

Area _____

683
× 5

Susan ordered 12 packs of pencils. There were 25 pencils in each pack. How many pencils did Susan order?

Color the number of cups it takes to make $1\frac{1}{2}$ quarts.

○ ○ ○ ○ ○ ○

○ ○ ○ ○ ○ ○

Fill in the missing number.

$$\begin{array}{r} \boxed{} \\ -\ \textbf{4.77} \\ \hline \textbf{4.77} \end{array}$$

$\dfrac{4}{9}$ ◯ $\dfrac{1}{3}$

Write all the names this quadrilateral could be called.

☐

_____

_____

_____

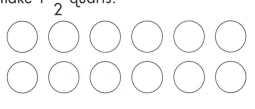

+ 1.7

1.3 ⟹ _____

3.5 ⟹ _____

2.8 ⟹ _____

2.3 ⟹ _____

4.6 ⟹ _____

7.3 ⟹ _____

1.7 ⟹ _____

6.2 ⟹ _____

Color the path of equivalence from start to finish without diagonal movement.

Start: $\frac{1}{3}$	$\frac{4}{5}$	$\frac{7}{9}$
$\frac{3}{9}$	$\frac{7}{10}$	$\frac{8}{16}$
$\frac{2}{6}$	$\frac{10}{30}$	$\frac{8}{24}$
$\frac{3}{10}$	$\frac{1}{2}$	$\frac{5}{15}$
$\frac{4}{8}$	$\frac{2}{3}$	Finish!

Write as a decimal.

seven thousand six hundred forty-two and nine tenths

$789.2 \div 10 =$ _____

 $- 9 = 54$

$54 \div$ $= 9$

Color the circles that are less than or equal to 32.67.

(32.8) (33.01) (32.8) (31.99) (32.200)

(32.499) (32.5) (32.670) (32.680) (32.098)

(33.1) (32.1) (32.111) (32.7) (32.607)

Round 345.622 to the nearest tenth.

- ◯ 345.7
- ◯ 345.6
- ◯ 345.62
- ◯ 350

Rule: +2	Rule: +2	Ordered Pair
0	0	(0, 0)

What time will it be in $4\frac{2}{3}$ hours?

_____

Hamburger	$3.49
Roast Beef Sandwich	$3.19
Grilled Cheese	$2.70
Add Fries and a Drink	$1.70

Courtney ordered lunch for her coworkers. Three people ordered hamburgers with fries and a drink. Two people ordered grilled cheese with fries and a drink. One person ordered only the roast beef sandwich and Courtney ordered the roast beef sandwich with fries and a drink. How much will the total bill be?

$$\begin{array}{r} 750.1 \\ -\ 32.98 \\ \hline \end{array}$$

Fill in the missing number.

$$\begin{array}{r} \boxed{} \\ +\ 6.4 \\ \hline 10.0 \end{array}$$

Jose's class of 26 students sit in groups of 6 at the cafeteria tables. How many tables will Jose's class fill up completely?

Rule: Multiply by 10

0.78, _____, _____, _____, _____

Write 7,062.891 in expanded form.

Fill in the missing numbers. Add two numbers beside each other to get the number above them.

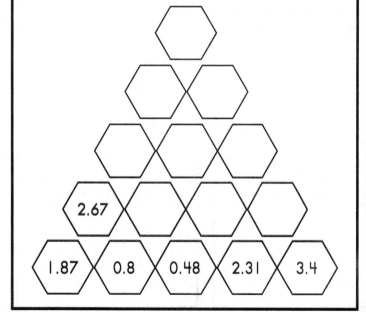

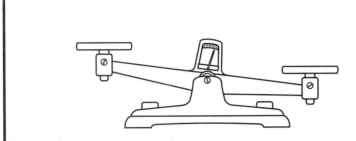

Write one of the measurements on each side to make the scale true.

2,500 pounds   3 tons

Which of the following is not a parallelogram?

○ rhombus

○ square

○ rectangle

○ trapezoid

Word Form

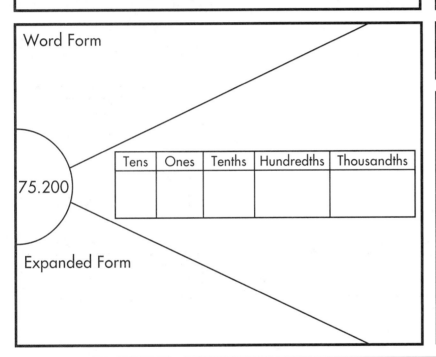

Tens	Ones	Tenths	Hundredths	Thousandths

75.200

Expanded Form

1 qt. ◯ 4 c.

Write 251.171 in word form.

6) 4,805

One pound of peanut-butter fudge is divided into ten equal pieces. How much does each piece weigh? Show your work.

2,489.846
Round to the nearest

hundredth. _____

tenth. _____

whole number. _____

$\frac{9}{10}$ ◯ $\frac{75}{100}$

Which of the following is equal to twenty-six thousandths?

○ 26,000   ○ 0.26

○ 2,600   ○ 0.026

Put the measurements in order from least to greatest.

8 c., 8 gal., 8 qt., 8 pt.

_____, _____, _____, _____

Write an expression.
3 times more than y

Johnna needs $3\frac{1}{2}$ cups of flour to make a birthday cake for her friend. She only has $1\frac{1}{3}$ cups of flour. How much flour does Johnna still need to make the cake?

Write the decimal for the shaded part.

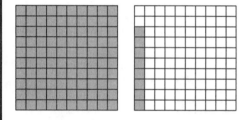

_____

0.44 ◯ 0.439

Circle the multiples of 6.

48, 74, 56, 60, 26

Millimeters	Meters
2,000	
	5
	8
	9
	11

327
× 3

Ms. Barker's class of 24 students collected milk cartons for an art project. If each student brought in 11 cartons, how many cartons did the entire class bring in?

Write a fraction describing 30 seashells for 8 grandchildren. If possible, reduce the fraction to lowest terms.

What is the value of the the 8 in 4,723.08?

30, 26, 22, 18, 14, . . .

Rule _____

Which figure is a right triangle?

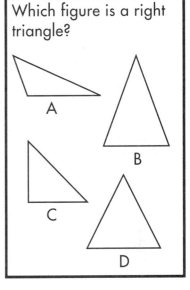

Round each number to the place of the underlined digit.

293.6̲55 _____

29.̲67 _____

1̲8.267 _____

4,56̲7.9 _____

2̲4.789 _____

Chairs were brought into the gym for the school talent show. They set up the left side of the gym with 8 rows of 24 chairs. The right side was set up with 6 rows of 20 chairs. Which expression could be used to find the total number of seats in the gym?

◯ 8 + 24 + 6 + 20

◯ 8 + 24 − 6 + 20

◯ (6 − 8) + (20 − 24)

◯ (8 − 24) + (6 − 20)

Solve the expression.

Write 203.401 in word form.

999.99 ÷ 10 = _____

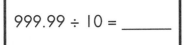

$8 - \bigstar = 64$

$64 \div 8 = \bigstar$

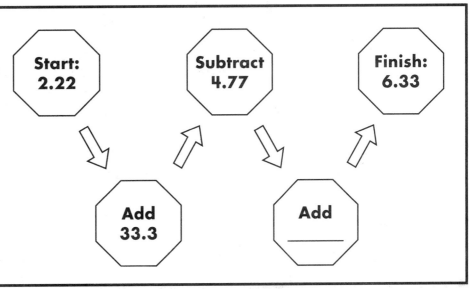

How many thousandths are equivalent to 5 tenths?

○ 50   ○ 500

○ 5,000   ○ 5

Solve. What patterns do you see?

77 ÷ 7 = _____	54 ÷ 6 = _____
770 ÷ 7 = _____	540 ÷ 6 = _____
7,700 ÷ 7 = _____	5,400 ÷ 6 = _____
60 ÷ 5 = _____	64 ÷ 8 = _____
600 ÷ 5 = _____	640 ÷ 8 = _____
6,000 ÷ 5 = _____	6,400 ÷ 8 = _____

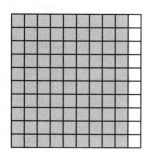

Write the shaded part as a decimal and a fraction.

fraction _____

decimal _____

$$7,911$$
$$-\quad 8$$

Round the answer to the nearest

_____

ten thousand.

_____

thousand.

_____

hundred.

_____

ten.

_____

$$42.9$$
$$+\ 4.78$$

What is the value of the 2 in 103.002?

The pet store ordered 112 bags of dog food. The delivery truck delivered 8 boxes of dog food. Each box must contain _____ bags of dog food.

The school is located four units left and two units up from the pet store. The school is located at ordered pair (____, ____).

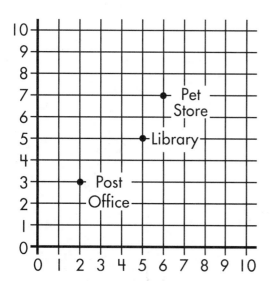

Rule: Multiply by 2

3, _____, _____, _____, _____

Add parenthesis to make the number sentence true. Show your work.

3 + 6 − 2 − 11 = 4

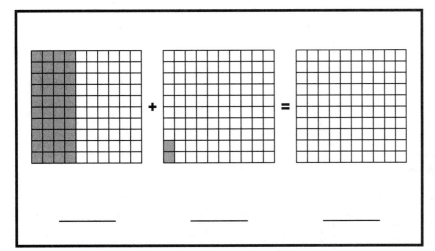

_____   _____   _____

Which statement is true?

◯ All quadrilaterals are squares.

◯ All parallelograms are rectangles.

◯ All parallelograms are quadrilaterals.

◯ All rhombuses are squares.

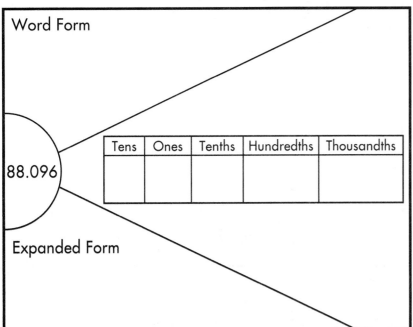

Word Form

88.096

Tens	Ones	Tenths	Hundredths	Thousandths

Expanded Form

48 inches = _____ feet

Use the geoboard to show $\frac{3}{16} + \frac{1}{4}$.

$\frac{8}{9}$ is closer to which benchmark number?

Color your answer.

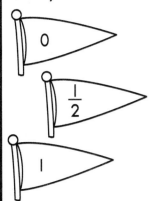

Place each decimal on the number line. Then, round to the nearest whole number.

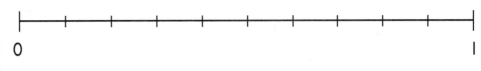

0   1

A. 0.8 _____   B. 0.20 _____   C. 0.5 _____   D. 0.70 _____

Write as a decimal.

four hundred eighty-six thousandths

$10 - \frac{1}{2} =$ _____

What decimal represents $(9 + 100) + (5 + 1) +$ $(8 + \frac{1}{100}) + (2 + \frac{1}{1,000})$?

- ⃝ 905.82
- ⃝ 905.082
- ⃝ 95.082
- ⃝ 905.822

Which decimal rounds to 2.5?

- ⃝ 2.42
- ⃝ 2.05
- ⃝ 2.59
- ⃝ 2.47

---

1 foot is _____ times as long as 1 inch.

In the last month, Davis has grown $\frac{7}{8}$ of an inch and his brother, John Paul has grown $\frac{3}{4}$ of an inch. Who grew more? _____

How much more? _____

How much did the brothers grow altogether? _____

Write the decimal for the shaded part.

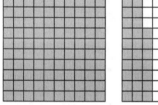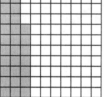

_____

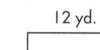
47.67 ⃝ 47.66

426 + 18.44

---

12 yd.

17 yd.

Perimeter _____

Area _____

7,458
×   9

Write an expression for the story pictured below.

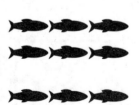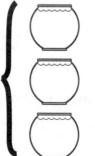

Name _____

How many inches does it take to make a yard? _____

Two yards? _____

Show your work.

Fill in the missing number.

$$\boxed{}$$
$$\underline{-\ 5.81}$$
$$2.32$$

$$\frac{12}{36}\ \bigcirc\ \frac{1}{4}$$

Write all the names this quadrilateral could be called.

_____

_____

_____

_____

– 0.5

0.8 ⇨ _____

1.5 ⇨ _____

3.7 ⇨ _____

1.6 ⇨ _____

1.4 ⇨ _____

4.9 ⇨ _____

6.7 ⇨ _____

3.3 ⇨ _____

Color the path of equivalence from start to finish without diagonal movement.

Start: $\frac{3}{4}$	$\frac{6}{7}$	$\frac{8}{12}$
$\frac{9}{12}$	$\frac{18}{24}$	$\frac{75}{100}$
$\frac{1}{5}$	$\frac{33}{44}$	$\frac{15}{20}$
$\frac{7}{21}$	$\frac{55}{60}$	$\frac{60}{80}$
$\frac{4}{16}$	$\frac{2}{3}$	Finish!

Write as a decimal.

eighty-eight and twenty-three thousandths

$47.84 \times 10^2 =$ _____

$12 - 7 =$ ✸

✸ $\div\ 7 = 12$

Color the circles that are greater than or equal to 99.6.

99.5   99.7   99.675   99.099   99.99

99.070   99.600   99.599   99.30   99.601

99.60   99.020   99.33   99.500   99.08

Name _____

Round 83.067 to the nearest tenth.

- ○ 83
- ○ 83.0
- ○ 83.07
- ○ 83.1

Stephen can't decide between a pack of 6 pairs of socks for $8.99 or a pack of 10 pairs for $13.48. Which is the better buy? How do you know?

Rule: +3	Rule: +2	Ordered Pair
0	0	(0, 0)

What time will it be in $3\frac{1}{2}$ hours?

_____

$$3{,}800.5 - 120.04$$

Fill in the missing number.

$$\boxed{} - 7.6 = 1.8$$

Round 2,884.208 to each place.

- hundredths _____
- tenths _____
- ones _____
- tens _____
- hundreds _____
- thousands _____

Rule: Divide by 10

70,000, _____, _____, _____, _____

Solve the expression.

$$(14 + 4) \div 3$$

Fill in the missing numbers. Add two numbers beside each other to get the number above them.

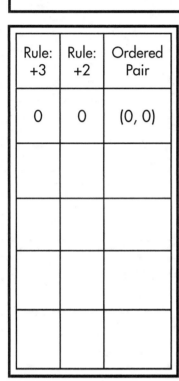

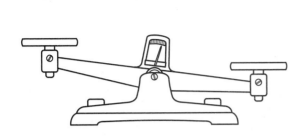

Write one of the measurements on each side to make the scale true.

10,000 g   12 kg

The driving distance from Elmswood to Porterville is 29.567 miles. What is this distance rounded to the nearest whole number?

○ 29 miles

○ 29.5 miles

○ 30 miles

○ 29.57 miles

Draw a line to match standard form with word form.

54.31   fifty-four and seven tenths

57.3   fifty-seven and three hundredths

54.7   fifty-seven and three tenths

54.031   fifty-four and thirty-one hundredths

57.03   fifty-four and three thousandths

54.003   fifty-four and thirty-one thousandths

825 mm ◯ 1 m

Which property of multiplication is shown?

(0 + 5) – 6 = 0 – 6 + 5 – 6

○ distributive

○ identity

○ associative

○ commutative

3) 9,037

Circle the point on the number line that represents $1\frac{1}{4}$.

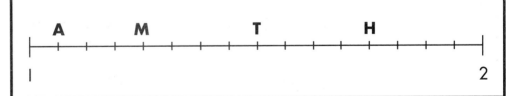

Tiffany spent $108 on 12 cans of paint. How much did each can of paint cost?

$\frac{3}{4}$ ◯ $\frac{5}{8}$

Circle the largest number. Underline the smallest number.

100.25, 100.1, 100.098, 100.3, 100.01

Put the measurements in order from least to greatest.

5 kg, 5 g, 6,000 g, 100 kg

_____, _____, _____, _____

Write an expression.
360 divided by s

Kris shared her pizza with Margie. Kris ate $\frac{1}{2}$ of the pizza and Margie at $\frac{2}{5}$ of the pizza. How much pizza is left over?

Write as a mixed number.

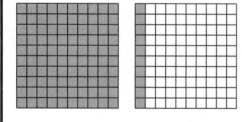

_____

63.635 ⬭ 63.636

$$905.29$$
$$+\ 84.91$$

Meters	Centimeters
	100
	300
4	
7	
8	

888
×   8

The shoe store received a shipment of 14 boxes. Each box contained 16 pairs of shoes. How many shoes were in the shipment?

A robin eats 3 worms every two days. At this rate, how many worms will the robin have eaten in two weeks?

Fill in the missing number.

$$\begin{array}{r} \boxed{} \\ -\ 2.05 \\ \hline 5.30 \end{array}$$

1, 3, 9, 27, 81, . . .

Rule _____

Write all the names this quadrilateral could be called.

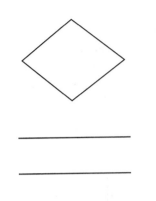

_____

_____

Round each number to the place of the underlined digit.

42<u>3</u>.86 _____

4<u>5</u>.98 _____

12.<u>7</u>1 _____

78.2<u>3</u>8 _____

238.<u>9</u> _____

The blocks below are stacked from heaviest (bottom) to lightest (top). All of the labels fell off when they were stacked. Write the correct label on each block.

| 4.1 kg | 2.20 kg | 7.8 kg | 7.03 kg |
| 4.10 kg | 7.030 kg | 7.80 kg | 2.2 kg |

_____	_____
_____	_____
_____	_____
_____	_____

Write 60.300 in word form.

$6.793 \times 10^3 =$

_____

$\bigstar \times 11 = 56$

$121 \div \bigstar = 11$

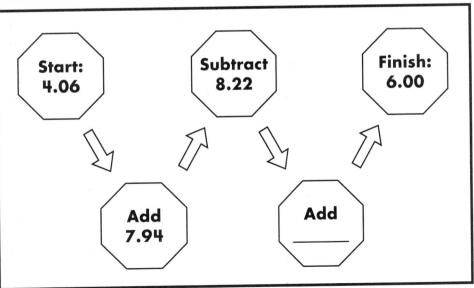

Start: 4.06 → Add 7.94 → Subtract 8.22 → Add ____ → Finish: 6.00

How many thousandths are equivalent to 70 hundredths?

○ 700   ○ 7

○ 70   ○ 7,000

Solve. What patterns do you see?

12 × 7 = _____	9 × 4 = _____
120 × 7 = _____	90 × 4 = _____
1,200 × 7 = _____	900 × 4 = _____
11 × 11 = _____	4 × 7 = _____
110 × 11 = _____	40 × 7 = _____
1,100 × 11 = _____	400 × 7 = _____

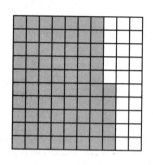

Write the shaded part as a decimal and a fraction.

fraction _____

decimal _____

7,650
×   8

Round the answer to the nearest

ten thousand.

_____

thousand.

_____

hundred.

_____

ten.

_____

0.75
+ 0.99

What is the value of the 3 in 2,458.039?

Fifty people are going on a rafting trip. If there are six people to a raft, how many rafts will the group need?

Rule: Multiply by 4

1, _____, _____, _____, _____

Add parentheses to make the number sentence true. Show your work.

11 + 6 × 6 – 8 = 39

Plot the points on the coordinate plane.

(5, 8), (7, 2), (7, 8), (5, 2)

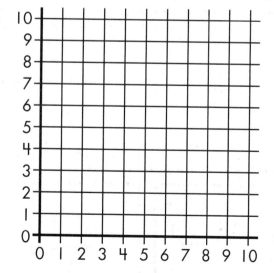

What is the perimeter of the figure? _____

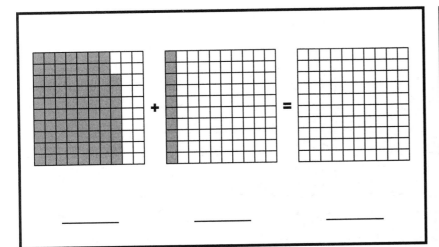

_____   _____   _____

Which number is equivalent to $10^4 \times 0.29$?

○ 29

○ 0.029

○ 290

○ 2,900

Draw a line to match standard form with word form.

11.1   eleven and eleven hundredths

11.01   one and one hundredth

1.111   eleven and one tenth

1.01   one and one hundred eleven thousandths

1.11   eleven and one hundredth

11.11   one and eleven hundredths

3 m = _____ cm

Use the geoboard to show $\frac{1}{4} - \frac{1}{8}$.

$\frac{20}{30}$ is closer to which benchmark number? Color your answer.

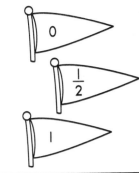

Place each decimal on the number line. Then, round to the nearest whole number.

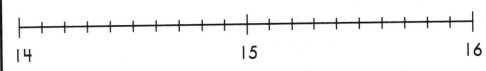

14   15   16

A. 14.5 _____   B. 15.70 _____   C. 14.1 _____   D. 15.9 _____

Write as a decimal.

$(9 \times 100) + (4 \times \frac{1}{10}) + (2 \times \frac{1}{100})$

$4 \times \frac{1}{2} =$ _____

What decimal represents $(3 \times 1{,}000) +$ $(4 \times 100) + (1 \times \frac{1}{10}) + (2 \times \frac{1}{1{,}000})$?

○ 340.12   ○ 3,400.12

○ 3,400.102   ○ 304.102

Which decimal rounds to 11.7?

○ 11.62   ○ 11.75

○ 11.77   ○ 11.67

I _____ is 60 times as long as 1 minute.

One lap around the track at the park is $\frac{1}{4}$ of a mile. Jose ran 9 laps. How many miles did he run?

Write as a mixed number.

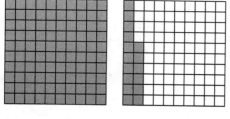

_____

19.707 ◯ 19.699

1,895
- 999

2 ft.

$5\frac{1}{2}$ ft.

Perimeter _____

Area _____

432
× 6

What is the measure of this angle? Choose the best estimate.

○ 45°   ○ 140°
○ 90°   ○ 180°

84

What is the value of p? _____

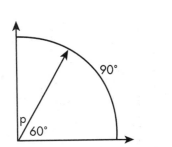

Fill in the missing number.

$$\begin{array}{r} \boxed{} \\ -\ 7.09 \\ \hline 1.50 \end{array}$$

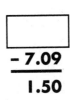

Circle the regular polygons.

Write as a decimal.

sixty-seven and eight thousandths

Color the path of equivalence from start to finish without diagonal movement.

Start: $\frac{1}{4}$	$\frac{4}{16}$	$\frac{1}{3}$
$\frac{3}{5}$	$\frac{25}{100}$	$\frac{4}{12}$
$\frac{3}{9}$	$\frac{3}{12}$	$\frac{4}{10}$
$\frac{4}{5}$	$\frac{5}{20}$	$\frac{8}{16}$
$\frac{6}{7}$	$\frac{20}{80}$	Finish!

〜 − 1.1 〜

1.8 ⇨ _____

3.7 ⇨ _____

2.5 ⇨ _____

1.9 ⇨ _____

2.0 ⇨ _____

9.4 ⇨ _____

6.6 ⇨ _____

1.3 ⇨ _____

$48 \times 10^4 =$ _____

 $\times\ 9 = 36$

$36 \div 9 =$

Color the circles that are greater than 0.208.

0.2   0.088   0.175   0.3   0.05

0.5   0.07   0.3   0.030   0.7

0.188   0.88   0.20   0.210   0.222

Round 419.197 to the nearest hundredth.

   ○ 419.22   ○ 419.20

   ○ 419.19   ○ 419

On Saturday, $2\frac{1}{4}$ inches of snow fell. The following Tuesday $\frac{5}{8}$ inches of snow fell. How much more did it snow on Saturday than on Tuesday? Show your work.

Rule: +2	Rule: +1	Ordered Pair
0	0	(0, 0)

What time will it be in $2\frac{3}{4}$ hours?

_____

   6.04
  − 0.85
  _____

Fill in the missing number.

   [   ]
  + 0.9
  _____
   4.7

Round 2,694.654 to each place.

   hundredths _____
      tenths _____
       ones _____
       tens _____
   hundreds _____
   thousands _____

Rule: Multiply by 10

4.879, _____, _____, _____, _____

Write 7,340.042 in expanded form.

Fill in the missing numbers. Add the two numbers beside each other to get the number above them.

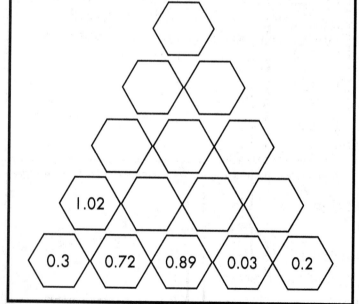

Name _____

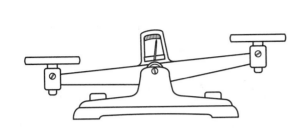

Write one of the measurements on each side to make the scale true.

15,500 pounds   8 tons

Which of the following is equivalent to 1,000 feet?

○ 333 yards

○ 333 yards, 1 foot

○ 3,333 yards, 1 foot

○ 333 yards, 33 feet

Plot the following ordered pairs on the coordinate grid below.

A (2, 7)   B (0, 2)
C (5, 1)   D (6, 4)

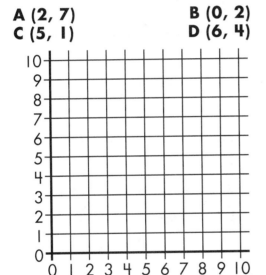

2 m ◯ 220 cm

Twelve people want to share a 42-pound bag of rice equally. How many pounds should each person receive?

○ 3.5 pounds

○ 4 pounds

○ 4.5 pounds

○ 4.75 pounds

6) 2,489

Kathleen and 6 friends are having a cookout. Kathleen bought 5 pounds of meat to share equally. How many pounds of meat are there for each person? Write your answer as a fraction.

A square fits in all of the following groups except which one?

○ rectangles   ○ quadrilaterals

○ trapezoids   ○ parallelograms

$$\frac{7}{12} = \frac{}{48}$$

Name _____

Week 18, Day 4

Which of the following is equal to nine and forty hundredths?

○ 9.40   ○ 940

○ 9.400   ○ 9.040

Put the measurements in order from least to greatest.

8 mL, 8 L, 9,000 mL, 5 L

_____, _____, _____, _____

Write an expression.
40 shared among m

Owen practices soccer for $2\frac{3}{4}$ hours every week. He spends $\frac{1}{2}$ of this time on dribbling. How much time every week does Owen spend on dribbling?

Write as a mixed number.

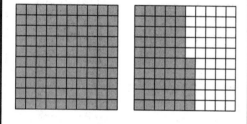

_____

42.300 ◯ 42.3

50.08
− 12.21

Millimeters	Centimeters
10	
20	
60	
	8
	10

78
× 8

The bakery received an order for 14 strawberry pies. The recipe for 1 pie requires 15 strawberries. How many total strawberries are needed to make the pies?

88

© Carson-Dellosa • CD-104885

150,000 minutes ◯ 100 days

23 weeks ◯ 150 days

30,000 minutes ◯ 2 weeks

Write a fraction showing 16 students for 3 tables. If possible, reduce the fraction to lowest terms.

22, 19, 16, 13, 10, . . .

Rule _____

Polygon	Sides	Angles
triangle	3	3
octagon		
pentagon		
rhombus		
hexagon		

Round each number to the place of the underlined digit.

660.82 _____

112.12 _____

457.95 _____

772.56 _____

9.04 _____

The blocks below are stacked from heaviest (bottom) to lightest (top). All of the labels fell off when they were stacked. Write the correct label on each block.

15.01 kg	15.1 kg	15.08 kg	15.10 kg
15.010 kg	15.8 kg	15.80 kg	15.080 kg

_____	_____
_____	_____
_____	_____
_____	_____

Write 1.053 in word form.

$0.3 \div 10^2 =$ _____

$4 \times$ ✦ $= 28$

$28 \div$ ✦ $= 4$

Start: 4.7

Subtract 4.7

Finish: 5.8

Add 2.9

Add _____

How many thousandths are equivalent to 3 tenths?

◯ 300   ◯ 30

◯ 3,000   ◯ 3

Solve. What patterns do you see?

84 ÷ 7 = _____	36 ÷ 9 = _____
840 ÷ 7 = _____	360 ÷ 9 = _____
8,400 ÷ 7 = _____	3,600 ÷ 9 = _____
121 ÷ 11 = _____	28 ÷ 4 = _____
1,210 ÷ 11 = ____	280 ÷ 4 = _____
12,100 ÷ 11 = ___	2,800 ÷ 4 = _____

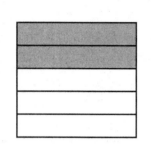

Write the shaded part as a decimal and a fraction.

fraction _____

decimal _____

True or false?

_____ All squares are rectangles.

_____ All rectangles are squares.

6,850 – 8.30	What is the value of the 5 in 100,500.02?

What is the value of *p*? _____

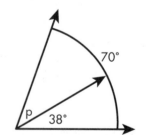

Rule: Add 12

24, _____, _____, _____, _____

Plot the points on the coordinate plane.

(5, 2), (1, 5), (1, 2), (5, 5)

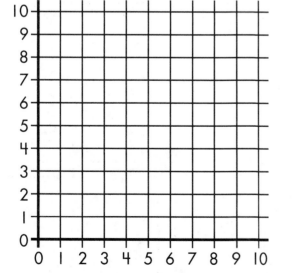

What is the area of the rectangle? _____

Add parenthesis to make the number sentence true. Show your work.

3 × 12 – 6 + 4 = 22

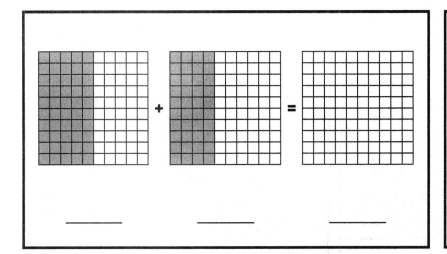

_____   _____   _____

Which number is equivalent to
$10^3 \times 2.46$?

○ 246

○ 0.246

○ 2,460

○ 24,600

Draw a line to match standard form with word form.

22.03   twenty and thirty-three hundredths

22.3   twenty-three and three thousandths

23.003   twenty-two and three tenths

22.003   twenty-two and three hundredths

20.33   twenty-two and three thousandths

23.23   twenty-three and twenty-three hundredths

2 gal. = _____ fl oz.

Shade $\frac{5}{16}$.

$\frac{9}{20}$ is closer to which benchmark number?

Color your answer.

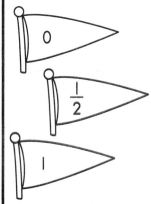

0

$\frac{1}{2}$

1

Place each decimal on the number line. Then, round to the nearest whole number.

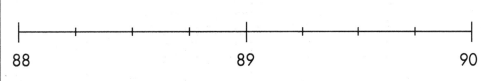

88   89   90

A. 89.250 _____   B. 88.5 _____   C. 88.75 _____   D. 89.500 _____

Write as a decimal.

$$\left(7 \times \frac{1}{100}\right) + \left(1 \times \frac{1}{1,000}\right)$$

$\frac{1}{4} \times 4 =$ _____

What decimal represents $(2 \times 100) + (1 \times 10) +$ $(7 \times \frac{1}{10}) + (3 \times \frac{1}{100})$?

○ 210.703   ○ 210.73

○ 201.73   ○ 21.703

Which decimal rounds to 13.2?

○ 13.55   ○ 13.29

○ 13.16   ○ 13.02

---

1 pint is 2 times as much liquid as 1 _____.

Zach and his family completed $\frac{3}{4}$ of their drive before having to stop for fuel. They completed another $\frac{1}{6}$ of the drive before stopping to eat. How much farther do they have to drive before they reach their destination?

Write as a mixed number.

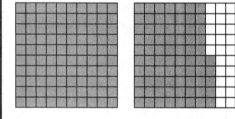

_____

108.308 ◯ 108.4

775.4 + 828

---

4 in.

$6\frac{1}{2}$ in.

Perimeter _____

Area _____

9,005
×   7
_____

What is the measure of this angle? Choose the best estimate.

○ 15°   ○ 120°

○ 90°   ○ 45°

What is the value of *p*? _____

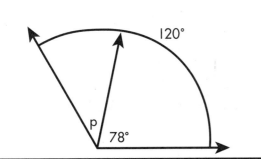

120°

p 78°

121
× 11

$\frac{1}{16}$ ◯ $\frac{2}{32}$

Circle the quadrilaterals.

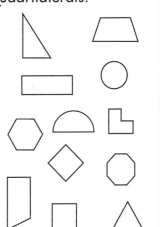

− 0.8

0.8 ⟹ _____

2.2 ⟹ _____

1.8 ⟹ _____

1.9 ⟹ _____

3.4 ⟹ _____

5.6 ⟹ _____

2.4 ⟹ _____

4.1 ⟹ _____

Color the path of equivalence from start to finish without diagonal movement.

Start: 0.5	$\frac{1}{3}$	$\frac{7}{15}$
$\frac{40}{80}$	0.75	$\frac{6}{10}$
0.50	$\frac{4}{7}$	$\frac{2}{8}$
$\frac{6}{12}$	$\frac{15}{20}$	$\frac{6}{30}$
$\frac{2}{4}$	0.500	Finish!

Write as a decimal.

twenty thousand four hundred and nineteen hundredths

$9.75 \times 10^2 =$ _____

$7 \times$ ✸ $= 49$

$49 \div 7 =$ ✸

Color the circles that are less than or equal to 0.4.

(0.375) (0.5) (0.078) (0.6) (0.022)

(0.410) (0.401) (0.400) (0.444) (0.004)

(0.40) (0.5) (0.388) (0.177) (0.8)

Name _____   **Week 20, Day 2**

Shade $\frac{1}{2}$ of 3 inches on the ruler.

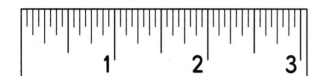

Martha is making cherry pies for her family reunion. Each pie requires $\frac{3}{4}$ cup of cherries. She has 6 cups of cherries. How many pies can she make? Explain your answer.

Rule: +1	Rule: +5	Ordered Pair
0	0	(0, 0)

What time will it be in $3\frac{1}{3}$ hours?

_____

7,900.2 – 238.55

What is the value of the 2 in 5,632?

What type of angle is this?

○ obtuse
○ acute
○ right
○ straight

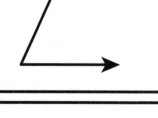

Rule: Divide by 10

1,110, _____, _____, _____, _____

Write 203.028 in expanded form.

Make your way from start to finish by shading only prime numbers.

Start	7	9	10	14
8	37	22	12	28
23	19	24	15	16
11	18	30	6	20
17	13	31	5	Finish

94   © Carson-Dellosa • CD-104885

Six cherry pies are set out for a party and cut into 8 slices each. If 36 slices are eaten, how many whole pies are left? Show your work.

How many grams are equivalent to 65 kilograms?

○ 0.065 grams

○ 650 grams

○ 6,500 grams

○ 65,000 grams

Draw a line to match standard form with word form.

8.78   eight hundred seventy-eight thousandths

87.8   eight and seventy-eight hundredths

808.7   eighty and seventy-eight hundredths

0.878   eight hundred eight and seven tenths

87.87   eighty-seven and eighty-seven hundredths

80.78   eighty-seven and eight tenths

2 gal. 9 qt.

Which property of multiplication is shown?

6 x 7 = 7 x 6

○ distributive

○ identity

○ associative

○ commutative

$$7\overline{)6{,}850}$$

The teacher has 60 minutes to tutor 4 students. If she spends the same amount of time with each student, how much time will each student have with the teacher?

Write as a decimal.

$$\frac{27}{100} =$$

$\frac{6}{11}$ ◯ $\frac{1}{2}$

A cake recipe calls for $2\frac{2}{3}$ cups of flour. Tiffany doesn't have quite enough flour so she reduces the recipe by half. How much flour should she use in the new recipe?

Put the measurements in order from least to greatest.

4 gal., 12 qt., 20 pt., 80 c.

_____, _____, _____, _____

Write an expression.
2 times the difference of 8 and 1

The turtle racetrack is 1 yard long. Pokey made it to the $\frac{4}{5}$ marker on the turtle racetrack. His competitor, Speedy, made it to the $\frac{3}{4}$ marker. Who went the farthest? How much further did he go?

Write as a mixed number.

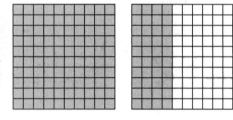

_____

0.179 ◯ 1.009

971 – 8.610

Kilograms	Grams
3	
5	
6	
8	
10	

$$\begin{array}{r} 2{,}050 \\ \times\quad 9 \\ \hline \end{array}$$

Jennie wanted to share a 64-pack of crayons with three of her friends. How many would each person get if Jennie shared them equally among herself and her friends?

$\frac{1}{4} + $ ⬚ $= \frac{7}{8}$

$\frac{3}{4} + \frac{1}{6} = $ ⬚

Fill in the missing number.

$$\begin{array}{r} \quad \\ -\ 0.83 \\ \hline 2.37 \end{array}$$

18, 36, 54, 72, 90, . . .

Rule _____

Circle the figures with parallel sides.

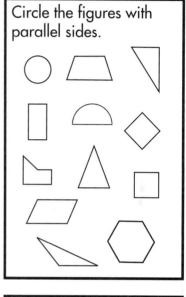

Round each number to the place of the underlined digit.

99.94 _____

329.04 _____

83.78 _____

966.44 _____

144.54 _____

The blocks below are stacked from heaviest (bottom) to lightest (top). All of the labels fell off when they were stacked. Write the correct label on each block.

| 0.25 kg | 0.05 kg | 0.2 kg | 0.050 kg |
| 0.20 kg | 0.250 kg | 0.55 kg | 0.550 kg |

_____	_____
_____	_____
_____	_____
_____	_____

Write 1,002.309 in word form.

$11 \times 10^4 = $ _____

$2 \times 12 = $ ✦

✦ $\div 2 = 12$

Start: 9.63

Subtract 8.52

Finish: 11.02

Add 2.5

Add _____

Use the models to find the product.

$$3 \times \frac{3}{4}$$

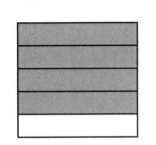

Write the shaded part as a decimal and a fraction.

fraction _____

decimal _____

Rule: _____

x	y
8	4
	8
18	9
22	

Solve. What patterns do you see?

7 × 7 = _____	12 × 2 = _____
70 × 7 = _____	120 × 2 = _____
700 × 7 = _____	1,200 × 2 = _____
9 × 3 = _____	4 × 4 = _____
90 × 3 = _____	40 × 4 = _____
900 × 3 = _____	400 × 4 = _____

8 + 3.62 + 8.9

What is the value of the 8 in 8.453?

What would the arrow look like if it were rotated 270° counterclockwise?

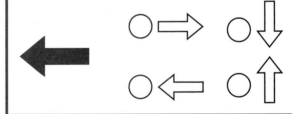

345.23 × 10 = _____

Add parentheses to make the number sentence true. Show your work.

7 + 42 ÷ 6 × 2 = 28

Add an ordered pair to complete the rectangle.

(7, 2), (3, 4), (3, 2) (____, ____)

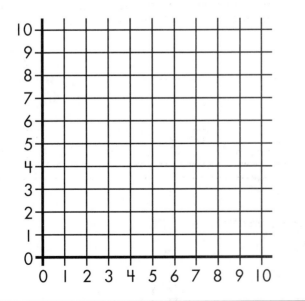

Name _____

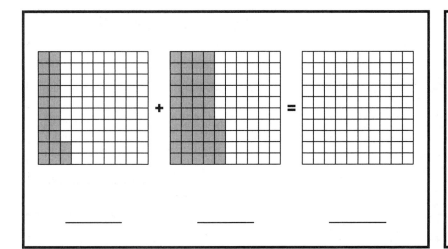

_____   _____   _____

Which number is equivalent to
$10^6 \times 0.005$?

○ 500

○ .500

○ 50,000

○ 5,000

Color the calendars to show 67 days.

67 days = _____ months, _____ weeks, and _____ days

6 pints = _____ cups

Use the geoboard to show $\frac{7}{16} + \frac{1}{8}$.

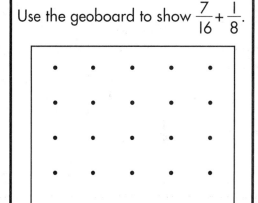

Find $\frac{5}{6}$ of 42.

(Hint: Find $\frac{1}{6}$ of 42 first.)

Place each decimal on the number line. Then, round to the nearest whole number.

99   100   101

A. 99.5 _____   B. 100.99 _____   C. 99.001 _____   D. 100.25 _____

Write as a decimal.

thirteen and four thousandths

$\frac{1}{3} \times 3 =$ _____

Which expression has a product greater than $\frac{3}{4}$?

- $\frac{1}{4} \times \frac{3}{4}$
- $\frac{6}{6} \times \frac{3}{4}$
- $1 \times \frac{3}{4}$
- $3 \times \frac{3}{4}$

Which of the following comparisons is not true?

- $34.34 = 34.340$
- $6.82 > 6.72$
- $89.304 > 89.5$
- $0.72 < 0.9$

1 inch is _____ times shorter than 1 yard.

Jase is competing in a bicycle race. He rode $15\frac{2}{3}$ miles before having to stop. He then rode $12\frac{1}{6}$ miles. How far has Jase ridden?

Round each number to the place of the underlined digit.

999.94 _____

150.05 _____

110.81 _____

60.828 _____

94.833 _____

5.030 ◯ 5.3

553.32 + 120.9

3 mi.

$7\frac{1}{3}$ mi.

Perimeter _____

Area _____

603
× 12

A bag of oranges weighs 2.8 kilograms and a bag of apples weighs 3,200 grams. What is the total weight of the fruit in kilograms?

Name _____   **Week 22, Day 1**

What is the value of p? _____

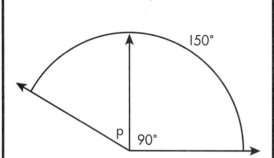

150°

p | 90°

---

2 (4 + 11) =

5 (18 − 6) =

$\frac{10}{100}$ ◯ $\frac{1}{10}$

Sketch a rhombus.

List the properties.
Sides:
Vertices:
Other:

− 2.2

3.4 ⇨ _____

2.5 ⇨ _____

4.7 ⇨ _____

6.1 ⇨ _____

5.4 ⇨ _____

3.0 ⇨ _____

8.6 ⇨ _____

3.3 ⇨ _____

Color the path of equivalence from start to finish without diagonal movement.

Start: $\frac{10}{50}$	$\frac{1}{5}$	$\frac{2}{10}$
$\frac{5}{6}$	$\frac{2}{3}$	$\frac{4}{20}$
0.4	$\frac{3}{4}$	$\frac{8}{40}$
$\frac{1}{4}$	$\frac{25}{100}$	0.2
$\frac{6}{8}$	0.25	Finish!

Write as a decimal.

forty-nine and one hundred thirteen thousandths

$23.4 \div 10^2 =$ _____

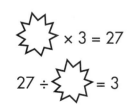 × 3 = 27

27 ÷ = 3

Color the circles that are less than or equal to 0.5.

(0.05) (0.8) (0.56) (0.9) (0.07)

(0.49) (0.50) (0.75) (0.4) (0.10)

(0.88) (0.09) (0.33) (0.01) (0.6)

Use the models to find the product.

$$2 \times \frac{2}{3} = \underline{\hspace{2cm}}$$

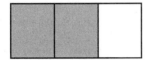 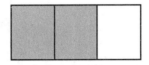

Brad's tree farm is busy planting new seedlings. They planted 42 trees in each of the 75 rows. How many seedlings did they plant? Show your work.

Rule: +3	Rule: +4	Ordered Pair
0	0	(0, 0)

What time will it be in $4\frac{1}{3}$ hours?

_____

8.9 + 3 + 22.22 =

$$\begin{array}{r} \frac{5}{6} \\ \frac{1}{3} \\ + \quad \overline{} \\ \end{array}$$

$$\begin{array}{r} \frac{5}{6} \\[2pt] +\ \frac{1}{3} \\ \hline \end{array}$$

What type of angle is this?

◯ obtuse
◯ acute
◯ right
◯ straight

Rule: Multiply by 10

5.83, _____, _____, _____, _____

Write 2,253.026 in expanded form.

What is the *y*-coordinate value of point Q in the figure below? _____

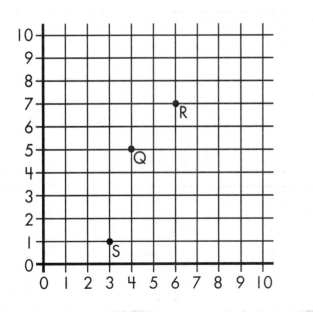

Name _____

Week 22, Day 3

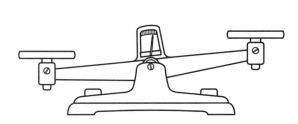

Write one of the measurements on each side to make the scale true.

18 kg   19,000 g

Which equation illustrates the identity property of multiplication?

○ 7 × 9 = 9 × 7

○ (7 × 9) × 3 = 7 × (9 × 3)

○ 9 × 1 = 1 × 9

○ 7 × 1 = 7

Draw a line to match standard form with word form.

9.89   nine and nine hundredths

99.8   ninety-nine and eight tenths

9.08   nine and eighty-nine hundredths

0.998   nine hundred ninety-eight thousandths

90.09   ninety-nine and eight tenths

9.09   ninety and nine hundredths

24 fl oz. ◯ 3 c.

Which property of multiplication is shown?

0 = 0 × 5

○ distributive

○ identity

○ zero

○ commutative

8)‾4,064

The chef made 3 pounds of pizza dough for 12 pizzas. How much dough is used for one pizza?

Compare without multiplying.

2 ◯ 2 × $\frac{1}{3}$

$\frac{1}{6}$ ◯ $\frac{3}{12}$

© Carson-Dellosa • CD-104885

Bradley had $\frac{3}{4}$ of a pizza left over after the party. For lunch the next day, Bradley ate $\frac{2}{3}$ of the leftover pizza. How much of the original whole pizza did Bradley eat for lunch?

Put the measurements in order from least to greatest.

36 in., $2\frac{1}{2}$ yd., $\frac{1}{2}$ yd., 4 ft.

_____, _____, _____, _____

Write an expression.
15 divided by the sum of 2 and 3

Marta and her uncle were installing a new floor in the dining room. Before lunch, they completed $\frac{1}{4}$ of the room. After lunch, they finished another $\frac{3}{8}$ of the room. How much of the room have they completed?

Write each mixed number as a decimal.

$2\frac{24}{100} =$ _____

$1\frac{5}{10} =$ _____

$7\frac{675}{1000} =$ _____

$9\frac{55}{100} =$ _____

67.67 $\bigcirc$ 67.7

486.29
− 221.83

Milligrams	Grams
	1
	3
	4
	7
	8

1,704
× 24

Carlos's work truck weighs 2 tons. His car weighs 1,200 pounds. How much more does his truck weigh than his car?

Convert the measurement.

300 km =

_____ m

_____ cm

_____ mm

Fill in the missing number.

$$\begin{array}{r} \boxed{} \\ -\ 7.18 \\ \hline 1.11 \end{array}$$

4, 8, 16, 32, 64, . . .

Rule _____

Circle the figures with perpendicular sides.

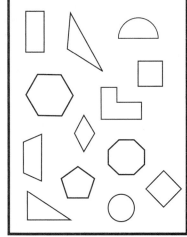

Round each number to the place of the underlined digit.

7̲77.45 _____

6̲7.98 _____

218.2̲88 _____

908̲.74 _____

67.80̲7 _____

The blocks below are stacked from heaviest (bottom) to lightest (top). All of the labels fell off when they were stacked. Write the correct label on each block.

| 4.11 kg | 4.01 kg | 41.1 kg | 4.010 kg |
| 41.10 kg | 41.11 kg | 4.110 kg | 41.110 kg |

_____	_____
_____	_____
_____	_____
_____	_____

Write 8,307.3 in word form.

0.73 × 10² = _____

---

4 × 4 = ☆

☆ ÷ 4 = 4

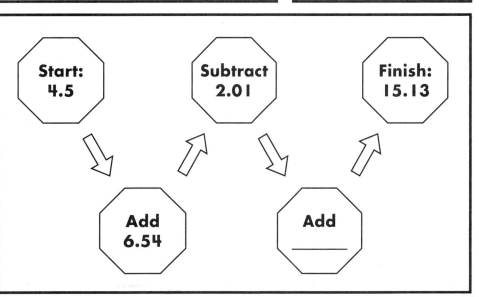

Start: 4.5

Add 6.54

Subtract 2.01

Add _____

Finish: 15.13

Name _____

Use the models to find the product.

$$3 \times \frac{3}{5} = \underline{\hspace{2cm}}$$

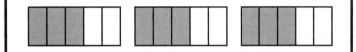

4,809
×   9

Round the answer to the nearest

ten thousand.

_____

thousand.

_____

hundred.

_____

ten.

_____

Rule: _____

x	y
27	9
	8
12	4
	12

Solve. What patterns do you see?

49 ÷ 7 = _____	24 ÷ 2 = _____
490 ÷ 7 = _____	240 ÷ 2 = _____
4,900 ÷ 7 = _____	2,400 ÷ 2 = _____
27 ÷ 3 = _____	16 ÷ 4 = _____
270 ÷ 3 = _____	160 ÷ 4 = _____
2,700 ÷ 3 = _____	1,600 ÷ 4 = _____

7.3 + 12 + 8.70

What is the value of the 6 in 365.409?

What would the arrow look like if it were rotated 270° counterclockwise?

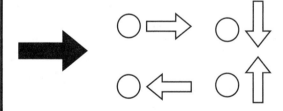

345.23 ÷ 10 = _____

Add parentheses to make the number sentence true. Show your work.

8 × 4 + 8 ÷ 2 = 36

Plot a point at (3,6). Move down four units and left two units. Plot a point. The ordered pair for the new point is (____, ____).

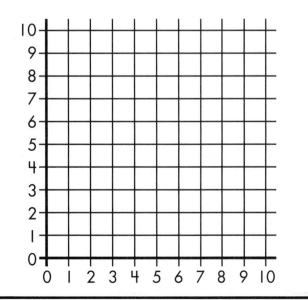

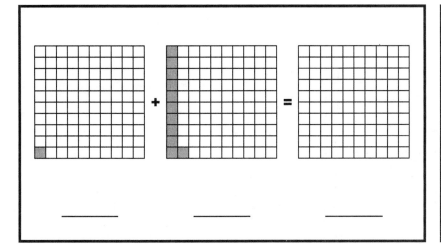

_____   _____   _____

Thirty-nine people have a meeting on the 18th floor of the Willis Tower. Only nine people can fit on the elevator at one time. How many trips to the 18th floor will the elevator have to make?

○ 3   ○ 5

○ 4   ○ 6

Use the data to complete the line plot.

$1\frac{1}{2}$, 2, 2, 1, $2\frac{1}{2}$, 3, 2, 1, $1\frac{1}{2}$, $2\frac{1}{2}$, 3, 2, 1, $1\frac{1}{2}$

1          $1\frac{1}{2}$ _____ $2\frac{1}{2}$ 3

Amount of Strawberries Picked (lbs.)

11.4 m = _____ cm

Shade $\frac{9}{16}$.

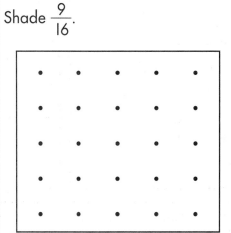

$\frac{20}{100}$ is closer to which benchmark number? Color your answer.

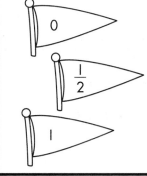

0

$\frac{1}{2}$

1

Place each decimal on the number line. Then, round to the nearest whole number.

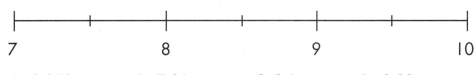

7   8   9   10

A. 9.250 _____   B. 7.01 _____   C. 8.1 _____   D. 9.99 _____

Write as a decimal.

twenty-one and ninety-five hundredths

$\frac{5}{6} \times 6 =$ _____

Which expression has a product less than $\frac{2}{3}$?

○ $4 \times \frac{2}{3}$ ○ $1 \times \frac{2}{3}$

○ $\frac{1}{4} \times \frac{2}{3}$ ○ $\frac{5}{4} \times \frac{2}{3}$

Which of the following comparisons is not true?

○ $0.4 = 0.404$ ○ $16.8 > 16.77$

○ $74.35 > 74$ ○ $99.3 < 99.40$

---

1 minute is _____ times as long as 1 second.

Derrick and Angela worked together on a school project. They each completed $\frac{1}{6}$ of the project separately. Over the weekend, they worked together and completed $\frac{2}{3}$ of the project. Are they completely finished with their project? Explain your answer.

Write each mixed number as a decimal.

$7\frac{9}{10} =$ _____

$12\frac{1}{2} =$ _____

$22\frac{25}{100} =$ _____

$1\frac{7}{10} =$ _____

$3,458.099$ ○ $3,458.1$

44,870 – 12,789.37

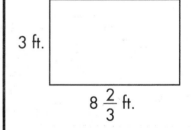

3 ft.

$8\frac{2}{3}$ ft.

Perimeter _____

Area _____

474
× 9
_____

The large crate held 396 dozen eggs. How many total eggs were in the crate?

Name _____

What is the value of _p_? _____

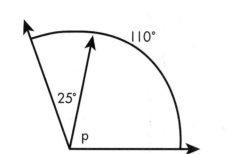

110°

25°

p

Fill in the missing number.

$$\begin{array}{r} \boxed{} \\ - \ 3.49 \\ \hline 1.79 \end{array}$$

$\dfrac{3}{7}$ $\dfrac{1}{2}$

What is the name of the angle that measures greater than 90° but less than 180°?

Draw an example.

- 0.6

11.2 ⇨ _____

2.6 ⇨ _____

1.7 ⇨ _____

0.9 ⇨ _____

1.5 ⇨ _____

2.9 ⇨ _____

3.7 ⇨ _____

4.8 ⇨ _____

Color the path of equivalence from start to finish without diagonal movement.

Start: 0.25	$\dfrac{2}{3}$	$\dfrac{4}{5}$
$\dfrac{1}{4}$	$\dfrac{1}{3}$	$\dfrac{2}{6}$
$\dfrac{4}{16}$	0.3	$\dfrac{4}{10}$
$\dfrac{3}{12}$	$\dfrac{1}{5}$	$\dfrac{5}{7}$
0.250	$\dfrac{5}{20}$	Finish!

Write as a decimal.

fifty-two and thirty-eight hundredths

$96 \times 10^6 =$ _____

$5 \times$ ⭐ $= 40$

$42 \div 5 =$ ⭐

Color the petals on each flower that are factors of the center number.

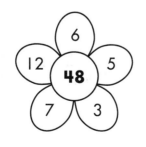

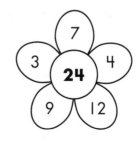

Use the models to find the product.

$$3 \times \frac{2}{3} = \underline{\hspace{2cm}}$$

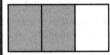 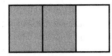 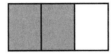

Rule: +1	Rule: +6	Ordered Pair
0	0	(0, 0)

What time will it be in $6\frac{1}{2}$ hours?

_____

The triathlon race next weekend consists of a $1\frac{3}{10}$ mile swim, a $56\frac{1}{2}$ mile bike ride, and a $13\frac{1}{5}$ mile run. How many miles is the entire race? Show your work.

**100.04 + 38.7
+ 14 =**

Fill in the missing number.

$$\begin{array}{r} \boxed{} \\ -\ 7.8 \\ \hline 0.9 \end{array}$$

What type of angle is this?

○ obtuse
○ acute
○ right
○ straight

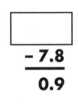

Rule: Divide by 10

98,700, _____, _____, _____, _____

Write 3,005.319 in expanded form.

What is the *x*-coordinate value of point L in the figure below? _____

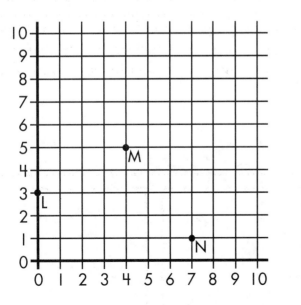

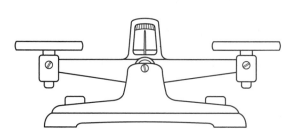

Write one of the measurements on each side to make the scale true.

8 tons	14,000 pounds
9 tons	16,000 pounds

Which mathematical expression is equivalent to this number sentence?

Subtract 15 from 45, and then divide by 3.

◯ $15 - 45 \div 3$

◯ $(45 - 15) \div 3$

◯ $(15 - 45) \div 3$

◯ $3 \div (45 - 15)$

Draw a line to match standard form with word form.

7.77   seven and seven tenths

0.777   seven hundred seventy-seven thousandths

7.7   seventy-seven and seven tenths

77.7   seventy-seven and seventy-seven hundredths

77.77   seven and seventy-seven hundredths

0.77   seventy-seven hundredths

5 feet ◯ 96 inches

There is $\frac{1}{4}$ of a birthday cake left over. If 4 friends want to share what is left equally, how much cake will each friend get? Show your work.

$9 \overline{)8,307}$

David made 22 ounces of lemonade. He and his two friends share the lemonade evenly. How many ounces of lemonade did each person get? Show your work. Then, round your answer to the nearest whole number.

Compare without multiplying.

$4 \times \frac{1}{4}$ ◯ 4

$\frac{5}{7}$ ◯ $\frac{1}{2}$

Daniel's flag football team has 24 players. Two-thirds of the team played last year. How many team members played last year?

Put the measurements in order from least to greatest.

2,200 lb., 1 T., 3,500 lb., 1 $\frac{1}{2}$ lb.

_____, _____, _____, _____

Write an expression.
156 decreased by b

Carter read $\frac{3}{4}$ of his book on Saturday. He read $\frac{1}{6}$ of his book on Monday. He finished his book on Wednesday. How much did Carter read on Wednesday?

Write each mixed number as a decimal.

$18 \frac{1}{4}$ = _____

$4 \frac{8}{16}$ = _____

$6 \frac{8}{10}$ = _____

$10 \frac{5}{100}$ = _____

1,000.04 $\bigcirc$ 1,000.2

$781.50
− $275.89

Liters	Milliliters
1	
	2,000
4	
	5,000
	10,000

6,853
×   16

At 6 am, the temperature was 68.8°F. By noon, the temperature had increased by 15.6°. What was the temperature at noon?

$\frac{1}{3} +$ [ ] $= \frac{5}{6}$

[ ] $+ \frac{1}{4} = \frac{5}{8}$

$$\begin{array}{r} 836 \\ \times\ 45 \\ \hline \end{array}$$

10, 100, 1,000, 10,000, . . .

Rule _____

Draw an equilateral triangle.

List the properties.
Sides:
Vertices:
Other:

Round each number to the place of the underlined digit.

1_17.230 _____

59_6.80 _____

8_0.563 _____

82.1_97 _____

9,8_76.7 _____

7,895 ÷ 10^3 = _____

6 × ✦ = 36

36 ÷ 6 = ✦

The blocks below are stacked from heaviest (bottom) to lightest (top). All of the labels fell off when they were stacked. Write the correct label on each block.

$\frac{3}{9}$ kg $\frac{2}{3}$ kg $\frac{8}{10}$ kg $\frac{15}{25}$ kg

$\frac{4}{6}$ kg $\frac{4}{5}$ kg $\frac{1}{3}$ kg $\frac{3}{5}$ kg

_____	_____
_____	_____
_____	_____
_____	_____

Write 802.203 in word form.

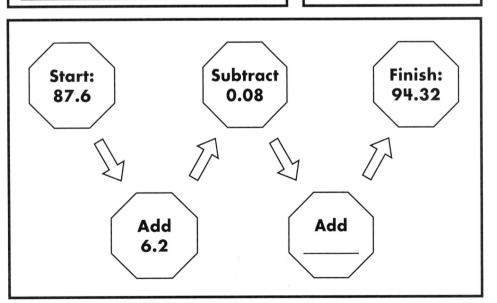

Use the models to find the product.

$$3 \times \frac{1}{2} = \underline{\hspace{2cm}}$$

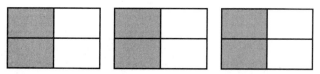

A small box is 5 centimeters long, 4 centimeters wide, and 3 centimeters tall. How many cubic centimeters would it take to fill this box without gaps or overlaps?

Rule: _____

x	y
3	13
33	43
8	
18	28

Solve. What patterns do you see?

8 × 5 = _____	6 × 6 = _____
80 × 5 = _____	60 × 6 = _____
800 × 5 = _____	600 × 6 = _____
9 × 7 = _____	6 × 8 = _____
90 × 7 = _____	60 × 8 = _____
900 × 7 = _____	600 × 8 = _____

$$\begin{array}{r} 7.99 \\ 3.37 \\ + 4.87 \\ \hline \end{array}$$

What is the value of the 1 in 87.129?

What would the arrow look like if it were rotated 270° counterclockwise?

$$78.362 \times 10 = \underline{\hspace{2cm}}$$

Evaluate the expression. Show your work.

$$2 \times [6 - (2 \times 2)]$$

Plot a point at (5,4). Move left two units and down three units. Plot a point.
Ordered Pair _____

10
9
8
7
6
5
4
3
2
1
0
  0 1 2 3 4 5 6 7 8 9 10

Name _____

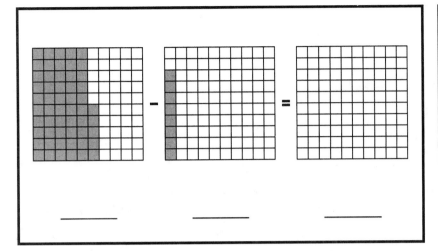

_____ _____ _____

Which of the following is equivalent to $\frac{7}{100}$?

○ 0.7

○ 0.07

○ 0.007

○ 0.700

Write an expression showing how many seashells would go into each bucket if they were divided evenly.

Shells Collected

5 am	10 am	4 pm	6 pm

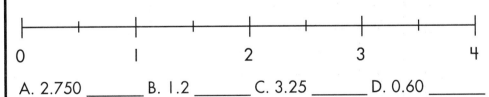

100 mL = _____ L

Use the geoboard to show $\frac{7}{16} - \frac{1}{4}$.

$\frac{8}{18}$ is closer to which benchmark number?

Color your answer.

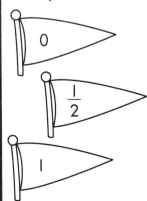

0

$\frac{1}{2}$

1

Place each decimal on the number line. Then, round to the nearest whole number.

0   1   2   3   4

A. 2.750 _____   B. 1.2 _____   C. 3.25 _____   D. 0.60 _____

Write as a decimal.

$(1 \times 100) + (2 \times \frac{1}{10}) + (7 \times \frac{1}{100})$

$\frac{4}{7} \times 7 = $ _____

© Carson-Dellosa • CD-104885

Which expression has a product equal to $\frac{7}{5}$?

○ $2 \times \frac{7}{5}$ ○ $\frac{5}{4} \times \frac{7}{5}$

○ $\frac{4}{4} \times \frac{7}{5}$ ○ $\frac{1}{4} \times \frac{7}{5}$

Which of the following comparisons is not true?

○ $707.07 = 707.070$

○ $14.197 < 14.2$

○ $3.349 > 3.200$

○ $78.8 < 78.708$

---

1 kilogram is _____ times as heavy as a gram.

Kaden went to the store. He bought $\frac{5}{6}$ pound of sugar and $\frac{1}{3}$ pound of flour. How much more sugar than flour did he buy?

Write each mixed number as a decimal.

$3\frac{2}{4} = $ _____

$6\frac{3}{4} = $ _____

$5\frac{25}{100} = $ _____

$12\frac{4}{10} = $ _____

7.89 ◯ 7.98

2,217.33 + 701.8

---

4 ft.

$9\frac{3}{4}$ ft.

Perimeter _____

Area _____

$\begin{array}{r} 371 \\ \times\ \ 8 \\ \hline \end{array}$

Barbara started watching a movie at 3:45 pm. What time will the movie end if it lasts $2\frac{1}{2}$ hours?

$\frac{3}{8}$ + 〔　　　〕 = $\frac{3}{4}$

$\frac{3}{4}$ + 〔　　　〕 = $\frac{15}{16}$

Fill in the missing number.

$$\begin{array}{r} \boxed{} \\ + \ \mathbf{5.6} \\ \hline \mathbf{7.44} \end{array}$$

$\frac{2}{3}$ ◯ $\frac{4}{5}$

Draw a shape or figure that would not be considered a polygon.

Explain why it is not a polygon.

Color all fractions equivalent to $\frac{1}{2}$.

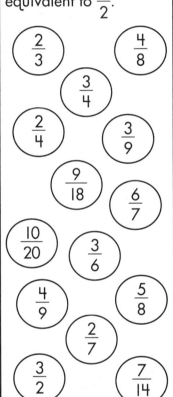

$\frac{2}{3}$ $\frac{4}{8}$ $\frac{3}{4}$ $\frac{2}{4}$ $\frac{3}{9}$ $\frac{9}{18}$ $\frac{6}{7}$ $\frac{10}{20}$ $\frac{3}{6}$ $\frac{4}{9}$ $\frac{5}{8}$ $\frac{2}{7}$ $\frac{3}{2}$ $\frac{7}{14}$

Color the path of equivalence from start to finish without diagonal movement.

Start: $\frac{1}{10}$	$\frac{10}{100}$	0.2
0.25	$\frac{2}{20}$	$\frac{2}{15}$
$\frac{5}{9}$	$\frac{5}{50}$	$\frac{7}{14}$
$\frac{2}{3}$	0.1	$\frac{6}{9}$
$\frac{6}{20}$	0.10	Finish!

Write as a decimal.
eighty thousand four hundred and nine thousandths

$111.111 \times 10^3 =$ _____

$7 \times$ ✦ $= 63$

$63 \div$ ✦ $= 7$

Color the petals on each flower that are factors of the center number.

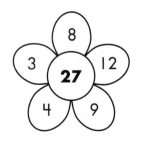

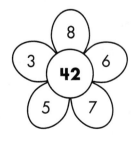

Name _____   **Week 26, Day 2**

Use the models to find the product.

$$2 \times \frac{2}{5} = \underline{\quad\quad}$$

 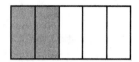

Rule: +6	Rule: +3	Ordered Pair
0	0	(0, 0)

What time will it be in $3\frac{1}{3}$ hours?

_____

They served hot dogs at parent night last week. Marty purchased 48 bags of hot dog buns. Each bag contained 8 hot dog buns. Four hundred thirteen people attended parent night. Did they have enough hot dog buns for everyone to have one? How do you know?

89 − 3.56 =

Fill in the missing number.

$$\begin{array}{r} \boxed{} \\ +\ 3.2 \\ \hline 5.0 \end{array}$$

Which type of angle is this?

◯ obtuse
◯ acute
◯ right
◯ straight

⟷

Rule: Multiply by 10

_____, 965.1 _____, _____, _____

Write 267.807 in expanded form.

Fill in the blanks to complete the area model showing 128 × 15.

	100	20	8
10	1,000	___	80
5	___	100	40

$$\begin{array}{r} 1,000 \\ \underline{} \\ 100 \\ 80 \\ +\ \ \ 40 \\ \hline \end{array}$$

118   © Carson-Dellosa • CD-104885

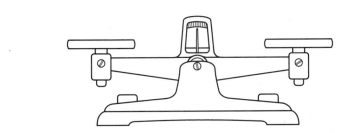

Write one of the measurements on each side to make the scale true.

| 12,000 g | 10 kg |
| 12 kg | 1.2 kg |

Which of the following is equal to six hundred thousandths?

- ◯ 0.600
- ◯ 600,000
- ◯ 0.006
- ◯ 6.006

Count the cubes to find the length, width, and height of the prism.

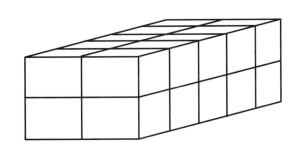

l = _____   *w* = _____   *h* = _____

6 lb. ◯ 80 oz.

Which property of multiplication is shown?

124 × 1 = 124

- ◯ distributive
- ◯ identity
- ◯ zero
- ◯ commutative

$8\overline{)5{,}902}$

Andre has 8 feet of yarn for a craft project. If he cuts the yarn into 6 equal pieces, how long will each piece be? Show your work.

Compare without multiplying.

$$\frac{2}{3} \times \frac{1}{4} \bigcirc \frac{1}{4}$$

$$\frac{3}{8} \bigcirc \frac{5}{7}$$

Jamie hiked 10 miles. He stopped to rest $\frac{3}{5}$ of the way through his adventure. How many miles did Jamie hike before he stopped to rest?

Put the measurements in order from least to greatest.

500 mL, 1 L, 2,500 mL, 3 L

_____ , _____ , _____ , _____

Write an expression.
the sum of 14 and p

Courtney made fruit punch for her birthday party. She followed the recipe below. How many cups of punch did she make?

Fruit Punch

$1\frac{2}{3}$ cups pineapple juice

$2\frac{1}{3}$ cups apple juice

$1\frac{3}{4}$ cups grape juice

Write each mixed number as a decimal.

$9\frac{6}{12}$ = _____

$7\frac{2}{8}$ = _____

$11\frac{11}{100}$ = _____

$13\frac{4}{5}$ = _____

18,057.3 ◯ 19,058.8

$799.99
− $275.33

Yards	Feet
3	
	15
7	
9	
	33

133
× 22

Susan saved $1,380 last year. If she saved the same amount each month, how much did she save in 1 month?

$\frac{5}{6}$ − ⎰⎱ = $\frac{1}{3}$

$\frac{1}{3}$ + $\frac{2}{5}$ = ⎰⎱

613
× 41

10,000, 1,000, 100, 10, . . .

Rule _____

Sketch a trapezoid.

List the properties.
Sides:
Vertices:
Other:

Round each number to the place of the underlined digit.

211.9̲8 _____

341.1̲19 _____

67.8̲9 _____

78̲.342 _____

8̲.789 _____

The blocks below are stacked from heaviest (bottom) to lightest (top). All of the labels fell off when they were stacked. Write the correct label on each block.

$\frac{10}{100}$ kg $\frac{5}{10}$ kg $\frac{4}{6}$ kg $\frac{1}{5}$ kg

$\frac{3}{6}$ kg $\frac{1}{10}$ kg $\frac{5}{25}$ kg $\frac{8}{12}$ kg

_____	_____
_____	_____
_____	_____
_____	_____

Write 4.829 in word form.

$898 ÷ 10^3 =$ _____

$6 ×$ ✦ $= 48$

$48 ÷ 6 =$ ✦

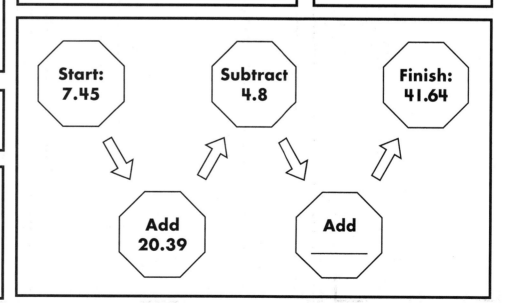

Start: 7.45 → Add 20.39 → Subtract 4.8 → Add _____ → Finish: 41.64

Name _____   **Week 27, Day 2**

Use the models to find the product.

$$2 \times \frac{3}{7} = \underline{\hspace{2cm}}$$

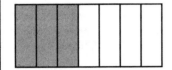 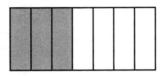

Solve. What patterns do you see?

40 ÷ 5 = _____	36 ÷ 6 = _____
400 ÷ 5 = _____	360 ÷ 6 = _____
4,000 ÷ 5 = _____	3,600 ÷ 6 = _____
63 ÷ 9 = _____	48 ÷ 8 = _____
630 ÷ 9 = _____	480 ÷ 8 = _____
6,300 ÷ 9 = _____	4,800 ÷ 8 = _____

4,221
× 12

Round the answer to the nearest

ten thousand.

_____

thousand.

_____

hundred.

_____

ten.

_____

Rule: _____

x	y
3	15
5	
8	40
10	50

902.04
− 272.33

What is the value of the 7 in 0.874?

What would the arrow look like if it were rotated 360° clockwise?

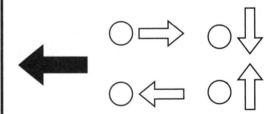

Plot a point at (2,1). Move right one unit and down one unit. Plot a point. The new ordered pair is (___,___).

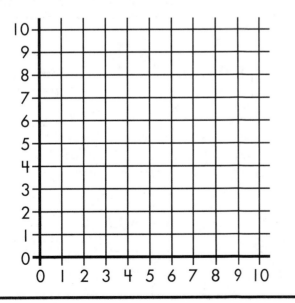

6,780.32 ÷ 10 = _____

Evaluate the expression. Show your work.

[5 − (9 − 4)] + 8

---

122   © Carson-Dellosa • CD-104885

Use the data to complete the line plot.

$2, 2\frac{1}{4}, 1\frac{1}{2}, 1\frac{1}{4}, 1\frac{1}{4}, 2, 1\frac{3}{4}, 1\frac{1}{4}, 2\frac{1}{4}, 1\frac{3}{4}$

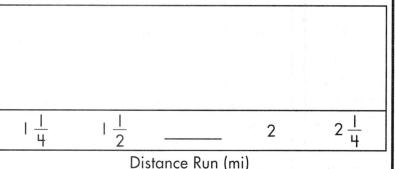

$1\frac{1}{4}$ $1\frac{1}{2}$ _____ 2 $2\frac{1}{4}$

Distance Run (mi)

It rained 0.37 inches on Saturday and 0.7 inches on Sunday. How much did it rain over the weekend?

○ 1.44 inches

○ 0.97 inches

○ 1.07 inches

○ 0.44 inches

Count the cubes to find the length, width, and height of the prism.

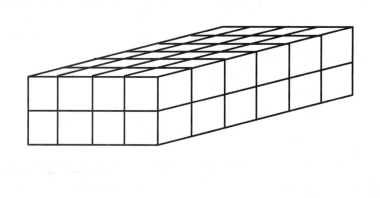

L = _____   W = _____   H = _____

---

280 mg = _____ g

Use the geoboard to show $\frac{3}{4} - \frac{6}{16}$.

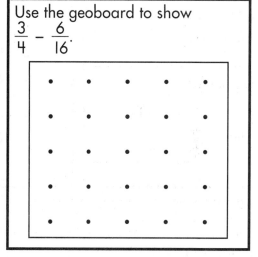

$\frac{80}{100}$ is closer to which benchmark number? Color your answer.

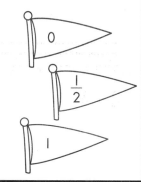

Place each fraction on the number line. Then, round to the nearest whole number.

41   42   43   44

A. $42\frac{75}{100}$ _____

C. $43\frac{25}{100}$ _____

B. $41\frac{1}{100}$ _____

D. $41\frac{99}{100}$ _____

Write as a decimal.

four hundred eighty-six thousandths

$\frac{1}{9} \times 9 =$ _____

Circle the largest number. Underline the smallest number.

111.45, 111.401, 111.4, 111.479, 111.48

Estimate the product by rounding each number to its greatest place value. Show your work.

$$\begin{array}{r} 294.7 \\ \times\ 39.62 \\ \hline \end{array}$$

I _____ is 1,000 times as long as a meter.

Carlos needs to get to the nearest gas station. Which gas station should he go to? How much closer is it than the other?

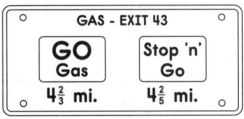

Write each mixed number as a decimal.

$27 \frac{3}{10} = $ _____

$5 \frac{4}{16} = $ _____

$18 \frac{8}{100} = $ _____

$27 \frac{57}{1000} = $ _____

$0.045 \bigcirc 0.009$

$$\begin{array}{r} 900.48 \\ +\ 378.72 \\ \hline \end{array}$$

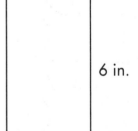

$3\frac{1}{2}$ in.

6 in.

Perimeter _____

Area _____

$$\begin{array}{r} 70 \\ \times\ 28 \\ \hline \end{array}$$

Lucy's class picked 156 apples at the orchard. If the class ate $\frac{1}{4}$ of what they picked, how many apples did they have left?

$\frac{7}{8} - $ 〰️ $= \frac{1}{4}$

〰️ $+ \frac{1}{3} = \frac{1}{2}$

Fill in the missing number.

$$\begin{array}{r} \boxed{} \\ -\ 2.3 \\ \hline 5.98 \end{array}$$

$\frac{1}{2}$ ◯ 0.47

Draw an isosceles triangle.

List the properties.
Sides:
Vertices:
Other:

Color all fractions equivalent to 1/4.

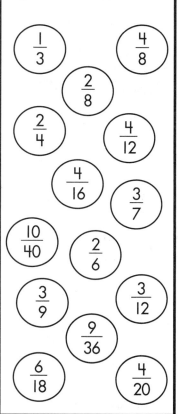

$90 \times 10^5 = $ _____

$12 \times 12 = $ ✦

✦ $\div 12 = 12$

Color the path of equivalence from start to finish without diagonal movement.

Start: $\frac{2}{3}$	$\frac{12}{18}$	$\frac{3}{6}$
$\frac{4}{12}$	$\frac{10}{15}$	$\frac{3}{5}$
$\frac{3}{15}$	$\frac{20}{30}$	$\frac{7}{14}$
0.4	$\frac{16}{24}$	$\frac{6}{10}$
$\frac{16}{20}$	$\frac{200}{300}$	Finish!

Write as a decimal.

two hundred thirty-one and five tenths

Color the petals on each flower that are factors of the center number.

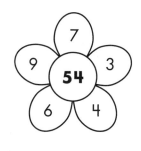

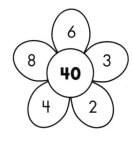

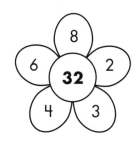

125

Use the models to find the product.

$$2 \times \frac{4}{5} = \underline{\hspace{2cm}}$$

 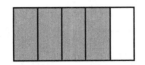

Race participants lined up in rows of 12 at the start line. If there were a total of 216 participants, how many rows of runners were there? Explain how you know.

Rule: +0	Rule: +2	Ordered Pair
0	0	(0, 0)

What time will it be in $1\frac{1}{4}$ hours?

_____

1,298 − 385.56

Fill in the missing number.

$$\begin{array}{r} \boxed{} \\ -\ 3.9 \\ \hline 0.4 \end{array}$$

What is the value of *p*? _____

55°
p
22°

Fill in the blanks to complete the area model showing 162 × 13.

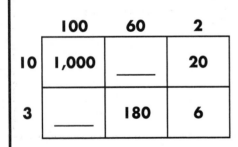

	100	60	2
10	1,000	___	20
3	___	180	6

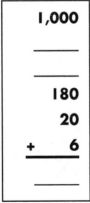

```
  1,000
  _____
  _____
    180
     20
  +   6
  _____
```

Rule: Divide by 10

_____, 7,100 _____, _____, _____

Write 830.122 in expanded form.

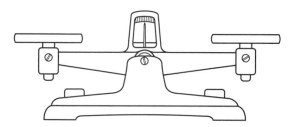

Write one of the measurements on each side to make the scale true.

17 tons	17,000 pounds
8.5 tons	8,000 pounds

Which pair shows equivalent fractions?

○ $\frac{4}{16}, \frac{1}{5}$

○ $\frac{1}{3}, \frac{8}{12}$

○ $\frac{3}{4}, \frac{9}{12}$

○ $\frac{2}{3}, \frac{9}{12}$

Count the cubes to find the length, width, and height of the prism.

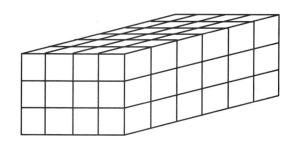

$l =$ _____ $w =$ _____ $h =$ _____

Volume = $l \times w \times h$

V = _____ cubic units

55 feet ◯ 20 yards

Which equation illustrates the identity property of multiplication?

○ $4 \times 1 = 1 \times 4$

○ $6 \times (9 - 4) = 6 \times 9 - 6 \times 4$

○ $9 \times 1 = 9$

○ $0 \times 12 = 0$

$4\overline{)3,333}$

Pedro bought 24 pounds of fish to feed 18 people at the fish fry. How many pounds of fish is that for each person? Show your work.

Compare without multiplying.

$2\frac{1}{3} \times \frac{1}{4}$ ◯ $2\frac{1}{3}$

$\frac{12}{30}$ ◯ $\frac{22}{40}$

Mary Catherine painted her room for $\frac{5}{6}$ of an hour. Her mom helped paint for $\frac{2}{5}$ of that time. How much time did her mom help her? Show your work.

Put the measurements in order from least to greatest.

200 m, 1.5 km, 1,000 mm, 10,000 cm

_____, _____, _____, _____

Write an expression.
3 times z increased by 18

According to the table, how much total rainfall has fallen? _____

Day	Rainfall
Monday	0
Tuesday	$\frac{2}{3}$ in.
Wednesday	$\frac{1}{6}$ in.

Write each mixed number as a decimal.

$6\frac{2}{5}$ = _____

$29\frac{60}{1000}$ = _____

$14\frac{9}{18}$ = _____

$2\frac{43}{100}$ = _____

0.3 ◯ 0.29

$$\begin{array}{r} 43.82 \\ -\ 42.57 \\ \hline \end{array}$$

Inches	Feet
12	
36	
	4
	6
	10

$$\begin{array}{r} 21 \\ \times\ 21 \\ \hline \end{array}$$

The nursery worker bought 26 apple trees to plant at $7.86 each. How much money did he spend on apple trees?

Name _____   **Week 29, Day 1**

$7\frac{7}{8} + 4\frac{3}{4} =$

$2\frac{3}{8} + 1\frac{1}{2} =$

$\begin{array}{r} 790 \\ \times\ 36 \\ \hline \end{array}$

512, 64, 8, 1, . . .

Rule _____

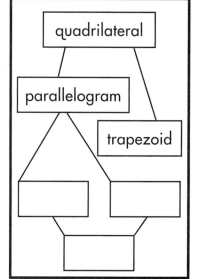

Round each number to the place of the underlined digit.

11 7̲.63 _____

8 9̲.521 _____

90 2̲.834 _____

29 9̲.69 _____

73 2̲.031 _____

$2938.4 \div 10^2 =$ _____

11 × 12 = ✶

✶ ÷ 12 = 11

What is the volume of the school locker shown below? _____

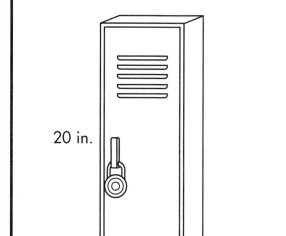

20 in.

6 in.
6 in.

Write 4,508.508 in word form.

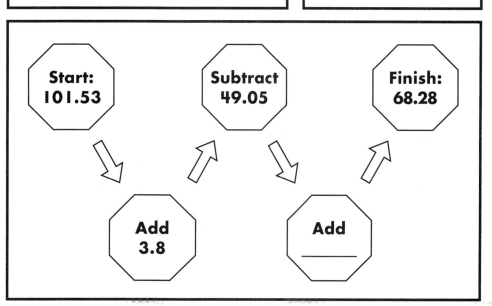

Start: 101.53 → Add 3.8 → Subtract 49.05 → Add ___ → Finish: 68.28

Use the models to find the product. $4 \times \frac{1}{3} =$ ___

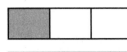

Solve. What patterns do you see?

12 × 12 = _____	12 × 11 = _____
120 × 12 = _____	120 × 11 = _____
1,200 × 12 = _____	1,200 × 11 = _____
8 × 10 = _____	9 × 9 = _____
80 × 10 = _____	90 × 9 = _____
800 × 10 = _____	900 × 9 = _____

4,503
×   13

Round the answer to the nearest

ten thousand.

_____

thousand.

_____

hundred.

_____

ten.

_____

Which box is heaviest?

Box A – 3 kg

Box B – 2,700 g

0.97
− 0.68

What is the value of the 3 in 678.983?

If 7 friends equally share 8 cookies, how much does each friend get?

Write the division problem that you would use to solve this problem. _____

Write the division problem as a fraction.

_____

Plot a point at (0,4). Move up two units and right three units. Plot a point. The new ordered pair is (___,___).

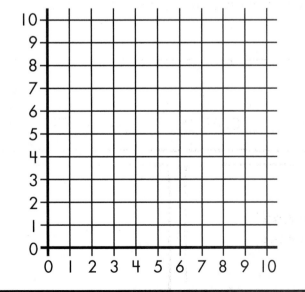

$1.802 \times 10^4 =$ _____

Evaluate the expression. Show your work.

[4 × (3 + 3)] ÷ 4

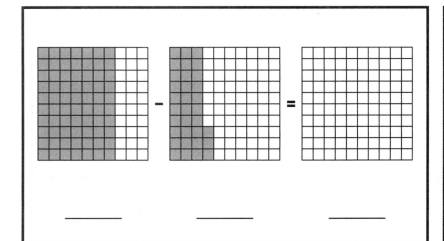

_____   _____   _____

Carlos drew a shape with five angles. Which shape did he draw?

○ hexagon

○ quadrilateral

○ rhombus

○ pentagon

Count the cubes to find the length, width, and height of the prism.

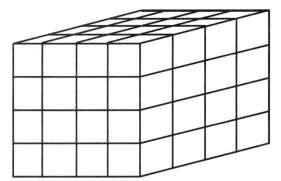

l = _____   w = _____   h = _____

Volume = l × w × h
V = _____ cubic units

15 km = _____ m

Use the geoboard to show $\frac{1}{8} + \frac{3}{16} + \frac{1}{4}$.

$\frac{22}{25}$ is closer to which benchmark number? Color your answer.

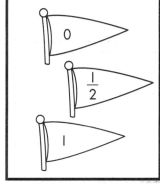

Place each decimal on the number line. Then, round to the nearest whole number.

67   68

A. 67.53 _____   B. 67.1 _____   C. 67.75 _____   D. 67.001 _____

Write as a decimal.

**seventy-one and
three hundredths**

$5 × \frac{1}{5} =$ _____

Which expression has a product greater than $\frac{1}{5}$?

○ $\frac{2}{3} \times \frac{1}{5}$ ○ $2 \times \frac{1}{5}$

○ $\frac{10}{10} \times \frac{1}{5}$ ○ $\frac{5}{6} \times \frac{1}{5}$

Which of the following comparisons is not true?

○ $5.6 > 5.600$ ○ $19.1 > 19.01$

○ $78.5 > 78.400$ ○ $10.19 < 10.23$

1 pint is _____ times as much liquid as 1 cup.

Jerry planted $1\frac{3}{4}$ acres in white corn and $1\frac{2}{3}$ acres in yellow corn. How much corn did Jerry plant in all?

Write each mixed number as a decimal.

$7\frac{4}{1000} =$ _____

$62\frac{3}{5} =$ _____

$5\frac{5}{20} =$ _____

$40\frac{1}{100} =$ _____

9.563 ◯ 9.603

2,310 − 456.73

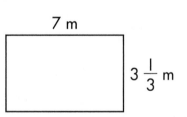

7 m

$3\frac{1}{3}$ m

Perimeter _____

Area _____

62
× 16

Annie poured 580 milliliters of soda from a two-liter bottle into two glasses. How much soda is left in the bottle?

$$3\frac{3}{4} + 5\frac{1}{2} =$$

$$1\frac{3}{7} + \boxed{} = 1\frac{13}{14}$$

Fill in the missing number.

$$\begin{array}{r} \boxed{} \\ -\,\textbf{0.9} \\ \hline \textbf{5.04} \end{array}$$

0.09 ◯ $\frac{1}{10}$

Draw a scalene triangle.

List the properties.
Sides:
Vertices:
Other:

Color all fractions equivalent to $\frac{1}{3}$.

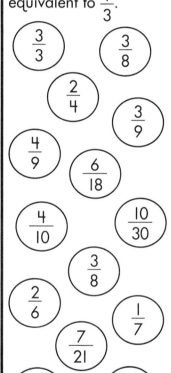

$\frac{3}{3}$ $\frac{3}{8}$

$\frac{2}{4}$

$\frac{3}{9}$

$\frac{4}{9}$ $\frac{6}{18}$

$\frac{4}{10}$ $\frac{10}{30}$

$\frac{3}{8}$

$\frac{2}{6}$ $\frac{1}{7}$

$\frac{7}{21}$

$\frac{6}{2}$ $\frac{4}{12}$

Color the path of equivalence from start to finish without diagonal movement.

Start: $\frac{4}{5}$	$\frac{40}{50}$	$\frac{3}{7}$
$\frac{2}{3}$	$\frac{8}{10}$	$\frac{1}{3}$
$\frac{6}{8}$	$\frac{400}{500}$	0.8
0.4	0.88	0.80
$\frac{7}{9}$	$\frac{5}{6}$	Finish!

Write as a decimal.

eight and four hundred five thousandths

$589 \div 10^3 = $ _____

$$10 \times \text{✸} = 80$$

$$80 \div 10 = \text{✸}$$

Color the petals on each flower that are factors of the center number.

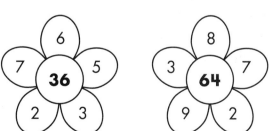

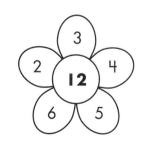

Name _____

Use the models to find the product.

$$2 \times \frac{5}{6} = \underline{\hspace{2cm}}$$

Rule: +2	Rule: +0	Ordered Pair
0	0	(0, 0)

What time will it be in $2\frac{1}{6}$ hours?

_____

Find the area.

3 cm

$1\frac{2}{5}$ cm

$\begin{array}{r} 32 \\ \times\ 0.8 \\ \hline \end{array}$

Fill in the missing number.

$\begin{array}{r} \boxed{} \\ +\ 3.6 \\ \hline 4.9 \end{array}$

Fill in the blanks to complete the area model showing 136 × 14.

	100	30	6
10	1,000	___	60
4	___	120	24

$\begin{array}{r} 1,000 \\ \underline{} \\ \underline{} \\ 120 \\ 60 \\ +\quad 24 \\ \hline \underline{} \end{array}$

If five friends equally share four bottles of water, how much does each friend get?

Write the division problem that you would use to solve this problem. _____

Write the division problem as a fraction.

_____

Rule: Multiply by 10

_____, 8.98, _____, _____, _____

$\frac{1}{2} \div 3 = \underline{\hspace{2cm}}$

How will the product $1\frac{3}{4} \times \frac{5}{8}$ compare to $1\frac{3}{4}$?

◯ It will be equal since the other factor is less than 1.

◯ There is not enough information to answer the question.

◯ It will be less since the other factor is less than 1.

◯ It will be greater since the other factor is less than 1.

Which pair shows equivalent fractions?

◯ $\frac{1}{2}, \frac{5}{9}$

◯ $\frac{2}{3}, \frac{6}{8}$

◯ $\frac{15}{45}, \frac{1}{3}$

◯ $\frac{1}{4}, \frac{4}{12}$

Find the volume.

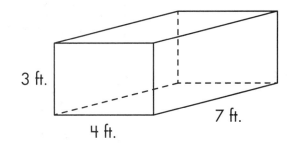

3 ft.

7 ft.

4 ft.

Volume = $l \times w \times h$

V = _____

---

6 gal. ◯ 16 qt.

Which equation shows the commutative property of multiplication?

◯ $7 \times 1 = 7$

◯ $4 \times 3 = 3 \times 4$

◯ $8(2 + 3) = 8 \times 2 + 8 \times 3$

◯ $0 \times 8 = 0$

$12\overline{)61}$

Bethany has eight minutes to complete 10 math problems. If she spends the same amount of time on each problem, how much time does she have for each problem? Show your work.

$1\frac{1}{2} + 2\frac{1}{3}$

Compare without multiplying.

12 ◯ $12 \times \frac{3}{5}$

Lexi bought $1\frac{3}{4}$ yards of ribbon. She used $\frac{1}{2}$ of the ribbon to make a bow. How many yards did it take to make the bow?

$$5\frac{1}{6}$$
$$-3\frac{2}{3}$$
____

Write an expression.
the product of a number and 8

Trent and his family went hiking. Trent and his father hiked the Mountain Loop Trail and the rest of his family chose the River Path Loop. How much farther did Trent and his father hike than the rest of his family? Use the map to solve the problem.

River Path Trail $1\frac{3}{4}$
Mountain Loop Trail $2\frac{3}{8}$

What is the volume of this object?

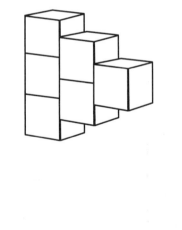

4.1 ◯ 4.01

1,508.8 + 342.18

The Smith family drove $312\frac{1}{2}$ miles on the first day of their trip across country. On day 2, they drove $278\frac{2}{3}$ miles. About how far have they driven so far? Show your work.

256
× 30

Estimate the sum of 0.59 and 0.53 by rounding to the nearest tenth.

Write an expression using all four operations (+, −, ×, ÷) that has a value of 10.

```
  603
× 27
```

32.1, 33.1, 34.1, 35.1, ...
      Rule _____

triangle

scalene   isosceles

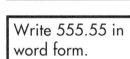

Round each number to the place of the underlined digit.

6̲7.823 _____

2̲39.32 _____

778.3̲49 _____

909̲.3 _____

8,002̲.34 _____

The blocks below are stacked from heaviest (bottom) to lightest (top). All of the labels fell off when they were stacked. Write the correct label on each block.

$\frac{50}{100}$ kg $\frac{2}{3}$ kg $\frac{1}{8}$ kg $\frac{24}{36}$ kg

$\frac{9}{9}$ kg $\frac{7}{14}$ kg $\frac{8}{64}$ kg $\frac{3}{3}$ kg

_____	_____
_____	_____
_____	_____
_____	_____

Write 555.55 in word form.

10 × 1,000 = _____

12 × ✸ = 36

36 ÷ 12 = ✸

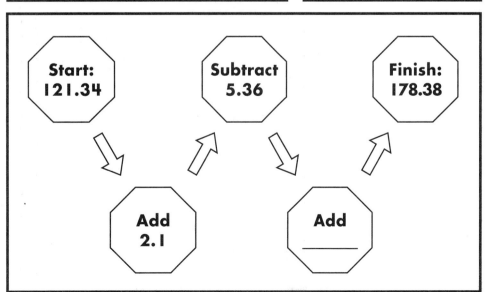

Start: 121.34

Add 2.1

Subtract 5.36

Add _____

Finish: 178.38

Find the product using the area model.

$\frac{1}{4} \times \frac{1}{3} =$ _____

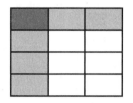

Solve. What patterns do you see?

$144 \div 12 =$ _____ $132 \div 12 =$ _____

$1,440 \div 12 =$ _____ $1,320 \div 12 =$ _____

$14,440 \div 12 =$ _____ $13,200 \div 12 =$ _____

$80 \div 8 =$ _____ $81 \div 9 =$ _____

$800 \div 8 =$ _____ $810 \div 9 =$ _____

$8,000 \div 8 =$ _____ $8,100 \div 9 =$ _____

6,023
× 15
—————

Round the answer to
the nearest

ten thousand.

_____

thousand.

_____

hundred.

_____

ten.

_____

Rule: $x + 4 = y$

x	y
3	
9	
4	
11	

0.4
× 9
————

What is the value
of the 8 in 9.781?

If three friends share four candy bars
equally, what part of a candy bar does
each friend get?

Write the division problem that you would
use to solve this problem. _____

Write the division problem as a fraction.

_____

Plot the points on the coordinate plane.

(1, 3)   (3, 1)
(5, 4)   (2, 3)

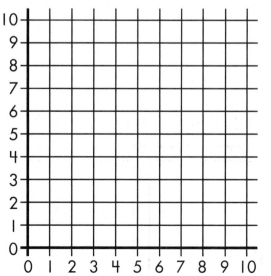

$33,000 \div 10^4 =$ _____

Evaluate the expression. Show your work.

3 × (5 × 4) − (4 × 3)

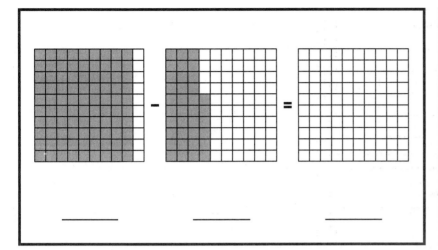

_____   _____   _____

The sum of $\frac{1}{10}$ and $\frac{1}{5}$ is between

○ $\frac{1}{2}$ and 1.

○ 0 and $\frac{1}{4}$.

○ 0 and $\frac{1}{2}$.

○ 1 and 1$\frac{1}{2}$.

Find the volume.

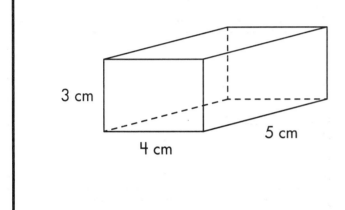

3 cm

4 cm

5 cm

V = _____

370 cm = _____ mm

Use the geoboard to show $\frac{1}{4} - \frac{3}{16}$.

$\frac{76}{100}$ is closer to which benchmark number? Color your answer.

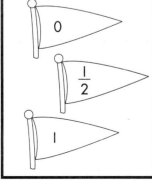

0

$\frac{1}{2}$

1

Place each decimal on the number line. Then, round to the nearest whole number.

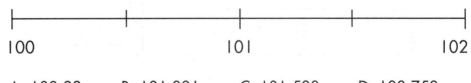

100   101   102

A. 100.33____ B. 101.001____ C. 101.500____ D. 100.750____

Write as a decimal.

(2 × 10) + (5 × 1) +

(4 × $\frac{1}{10}$) + (9 × $\frac{1}{1,000}$)

$\frac{3}{4} × 8 =$ _____

Which product will have 2 decimal places?

◯ 3 × 4.5   ◯ 2.34 × 0.17

◯ 1.5 × 0.88   ◯ 2.1 × 4.2

Which number is equivalent to 0.32×10^3?

◯ 0.32   ◯ 32

◯ 0.032   ◯ 320

I _____ is 10 times as long as 1 millimeter.

During football practice, the coach had the team work on offensive drills for $\frac{2}{3}$ of an hour. They then worked on defensive drills for $\frac{3}{4}$ of an hour more. How long did the team practice? Show your work.

What is the volume of this object?

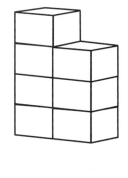

0.18 ◯ 0.9

```
  445.18
+  88.88
```

If 8 students want to share 6 candy bars equally, how much will each student get? Show your work.

```
  23
× 19
```

If a rectangle has a length of 8 centimeters and a width of 3 centimeters, find the area.

$\frac{1}{5} \times \frac{1}{4} =$ _____

Fill in the missing number.

$$\boxed{}$$
$$- \ 5.1$$
$$\overline{\ \ 2.66\ }$$

$\frac{1}{3}$ 0.4

Draw an irregular hexagon.

How do you know it is irregular?

Color all fractions equivalent to $\frac{2}{3}$.

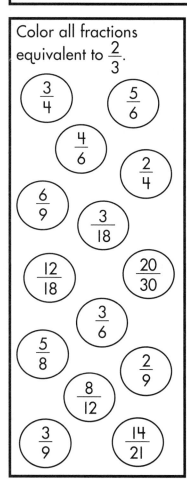

Color the path of equivalence from start to finish without diagonal movement.

Start: $\frac{4}{10}$	$\frac{2}{4}$	$\frac{1}{8}$
$\frac{2}{5}$	$\frac{14}{15}$	$\frac{3}{4}$
0.4	0.5	$\frac{2}{3}$
$\frac{12}{30}$	$\frac{20}{50}$	$\frac{5}{7}$
$\frac{7}{8}$	0.400	Finish!

Write as a decimal.

fifty and sixty-six hundredths

$1,000 \div 10^1 =$ _____

$9 \times 9 =$ ☆

☆ $\div 9 = 9$

Color the petals on each flower that are factors of the center number.

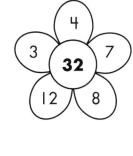
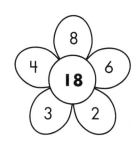

Find the product using the area model.

$\frac{3}{4} \times \frac{1}{3} =$ _____

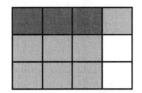

Find the area of the rug.

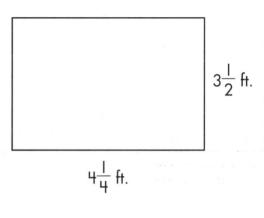

$3\frac{1}{2}$ ft.

$4\frac{1}{4}$ ft.

Rule: +4	Rule: +2	Ordered Pair
0	0	(0, 0)

What time will it be in $3\frac{2}{3}$ hours?

_____

14
× 0.5

Fill in the missing number.

```
  [    ]
– 4.1
─────
  0.6
```

Fill in the blanks to complete the area model showing 175 × 12.

	100	70	5
10	1,000	____	50
2	____	140	10

```
  1,000
  _____
  _____
    140
     50
+    10
  _____
```

Brianna used 1 cup of sugar to make a dozen cookies. How much sugar was in each cookie?

Rule: Divide by 10

_____, 1,101, _____, _____, _____

$\frac{1}{5} \div 2 =$ _____

How many cubic inches would it take to fill this right rectangular prism without any gaps or overlaps?

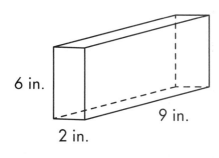

6 in.

9 in.

2 in.

_____

Which inequality is true?

○ $\frac{1}{2} > \frac{3}{4}$

○ $\frac{1}{5} > \frac{1}{3}$

○ $\frac{1}{8} > \frac{1}{4}$

○ $\frac{2}{3} > \frac{3}{5}$

Find the volume.

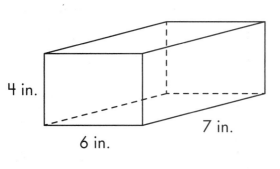

4 in.

6 in.

7 in.

V = _____

750 g 7.6 kg

A single bat can eat 950 mosquitoes in an hour! At this rate, how much could one bat eat in 8 hours?

In 24 hours?

In a week?

$9\overline{)1,611}$

Eight friends are sharing 7 pizzas equally. How much pizza will each friend get? Draw a picture to show your thinking.

Write as a decimal.

four hundred eight and eight thousandths

$\frac{1}{10}$ ◯ $\frac{2}{20}$

Xander practices soccer $3\frac{3}{4}$ hours a week. He works on defense for $\frac{2}{5}$ of this time. How many hours a week does Xander spend on defense each week? Show your work.

Which of the following is equal to eight thousand and sixteen thousandths?

○ 8,016   ○ 8,000.16

○ 8,001.6   ○ 8,000.016

Write an expression.
five more than twice a number

Nicholas read $\frac{2}{5}$ of his book aloud to his brother. He then read $\frac{1}{3}$ of it in the car. How much more does Nicholas have to read in order to finish the book?

What is the volume of this object?

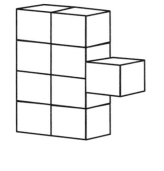

0.38 ◯ 0.380

611.49
− 176.53

Inches	Feet
12	
	3
	5
84	
	10

43
× 35

Estimate the sum of 6.299 and 5.402 by rounding to the nearest hundredth.

$\dfrac{2}{3} \times \dfrac{1}{4} =$ _____

526
× 25

$\dfrac{1}{8}, \dfrac{3}{8}, \dfrac{3}{8}, \dfrac{7}{8}, \dfrac{9}{8}, \cdots$

Rule _____

Sketch a robot using six regular polygons and six irregular polygons.

Round each number to the place of the underlined digit.

7,852.99 _____

670.4 _____

87.397 _____

12.994 _____

88.7 _____

The blocks below are stacked from heaviest (bottom) to lightest (top). All of the labels fell off when they were stacked. Write the correct label on each block.

| 0.5 kg | $\dfrac{1}{4}$ kg | 0.8 kg | 0.25 kg |

| $\dfrac{5}{10}$ kg | $\dfrac{3}{10}$ kg | 0.30 kg | $\dfrac{8}{10}$ kg |

_____	_____
_____	_____
_____	_____
_____	_____

Write 9,804.987 in word form.

$5,984.5 \times 10^3 =$ _____

$6 \times$ ⭐ $= 54$

$54 \div 6 =$ ⭐

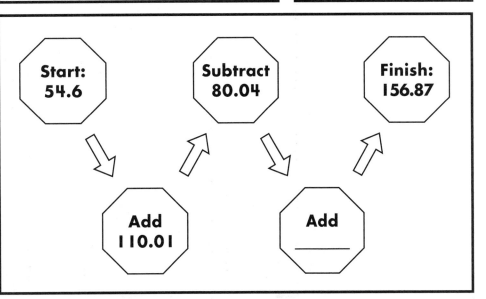

Start: 54.6

Subtract 80.04

Finish: 156.87

Add 110.01

Add _____

Find the product using the area model.

$\frac{1}{3} \times \frac{3}{5} =$ _____

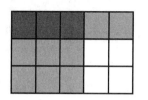

Solve. What patterns do you see?

5 × 7 = _____	11 × 4 = _____
50 × 7 = _____	110 × 4 = _____
500 × 7 = _____	1,100 × 4 = _____
12 × 6 = _____	12 × 9 = _____
120 × 6 = _____	120 × 9 = _____
1,200 × 6 = _____	1,200 × 9 = _____

11,400
×   11

Round the answer to the nearest

ten thousand

_____

thousand

_____

hundred

_____

ten

_____

Rule: $2x = y$

x	y
4	
2	
11	
9	

19
× 0.7

What is the value of 7 in 52.271?

Greg bought 6 ounces of deli meat. Each slice was $\frac{1}{4}$ ounce. How many slices did he buy? Show your work.

Plot the points on the coordinate plane.

(0, 5)   (2, 4)
(3, 1)   (4, 2)

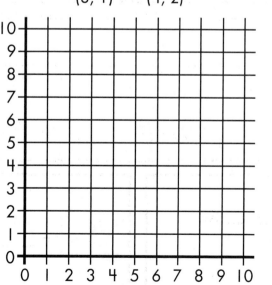

$0.005 \times 10^6 =$ _____

Evaluate the expression. Show your work.

(9 × 2) ÷ (14 – 8) × 3

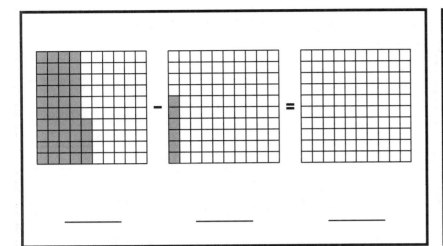

_____ - _____ = _____

Tiffany needs to measure the length of her bedroom. Which unit of measurement is most appropriate?

○ millimeter

○ inch

○ foot

○ centimeter

Find the volume of each. Circle the figure with the greatest volume.

V = _____

2 cm

V = _____

3 cm

4 cm

5 cm

130 g = _____ mg

Use the geoboard to show
$\frac{5}{16} + \frac{1}{8} + \frac{1}{2}$.

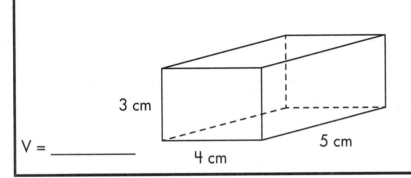

$\frac{10}{12}$ is closer to which benchmark number? Color your answer.

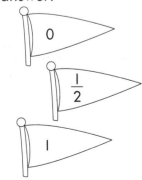

0

$\frac{1}{2}$

1

Place each fraction on the number line. Then, round to the nearest whole number.

|———————|———————|———————|
0   1

A. $79\frac{3}{4}$ ____   B. $80\frac{90}{100}$ ____   C. $79\frac{250}{1000}$ ____   D. $80\frac{25}{100}$ ____

Write as a decimal.

eight and eight tenths

$\frac{1}{3} \times 9 =$ _____

Which product will have 3 decimal places?

◯ 5.2 × 7.5   ◯ 4.15 × 0.37

◯ 87.5 × 0.66   ◯ 6.4 × 8

Which number is equivalent to 8.2×10^4?

◯ 820   ◯ 8,200

◯ 82,000   ◯ 0.082

---

3 yards is _____ times as long as 1 inch.

Last year, Mel paid off $\frac{1}{4}$ of her car. This year, she plans to pay $\frac{1}{3}$. After this year how much more does she need to pay to have her car completely paid off?

What is the volume of this object?

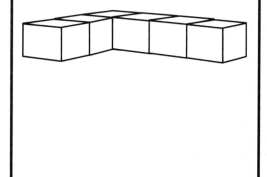

3.17 ◯ 3.017

$$\begin{array}{r} 87.32 \\ - 29.44 \\ \hline \end{array}$$

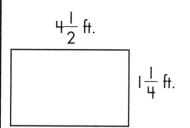

$4\frac{1}{2}$ ft.

$1\frac{1}{4}$ ft.

Perimeter _____

Area _____

$$\begin{array}{r} 71 \\ \times 41 \\ \hline \end{array}$$

Use order of operations to solve. Show your work at each step.

$$112 \div [(12 \div 3) \times 2]$$

$4 \times 3\frac{1}{2} =$ _____

Fill in the missing number.

$$\boxed{}$$
$$\underline{+\ 7.63}$$
$$9.00$$

$\frac{3}{4}$  0.8

Draw a parallelogram.

List the properties.
Sides:
Vertices:
Other:

Color all fractions equivalent to 1.

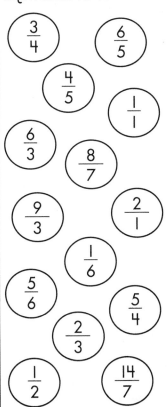

$\frac{3}{4}$ $\frac{6}{5}$

$\frac{4}{5}$ $\frac{1}{1}$

$\frac{6}{3}$ $\frac{8}{7}$

$\frac{9}{3}$ $\frac{2}{1}$

$\frac{1}{6}$

$\frac{5}{6}$ $\frac{5}{4}$

$\frac{2}{3}$

$\frac{1}{2}$ $\frac{14}{7}$

Color the path of equivalence from start to finish without diagonal movement.

Start: $\frac{9}{15}$	$\frac{6}{10}$	0.70
$\frac{3}{4}$	0.60	$\frac{2}{3}$
$\frac{4}{7}$	$\frac{3}{5}$	$\frac{12}{20}$
$\frac{1}{5}$	$\frac{5}{12}$	$\frac{30}{50}$
$\frac{3}{10}$	$\frac{6}{11}$	Finish!

Write as a decimal.

seventy-two and eight hundred five thousandths

$0.075 \times 10^5 =$ _____

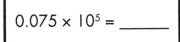

$7 \times$ ☼ $= 35$

$35 \div$ ☼ $= 7$

Color the petals on each flower that are factors of the center number.

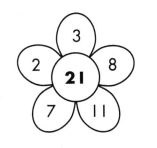
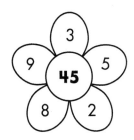
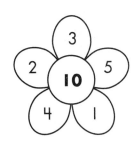

Find the product using the area model.

$\frac{3}{4} \times \frac{2}{5} =$ _____

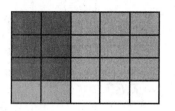

Find the area.

$4\frac{4}{5}$ cm

$2\frac{3}{4}$ cm

Rule: +1	Rule: +1	Ordered Pair
0	0	(0,0)

What time will it be in $1\frac{1}{3}$ hours?

_____

12
× 0.3
_____

Fill in the missing number.

☐
− 3.6
_____
7.2

Mikey mixed up 4 cups of muffin batter. If Mikey used $\frac{1}{3}$ cup of batter to make each muffin, how many muffins can he make?

The community competition pool is 18 feet long, 12 feet wide, and 8 feet deep. What is the total volume of the pool? Show your work.

The community kiddie pool is 12 feet long, 12 feet wide, and 2 feet deep. What is the total volume of the kiddie pool? Show your work.

What is the total volume of both pools?

Rule: Multiply by 10

_____, 2.11, _____, _____, _____

$1 \div \frac{1}{3} =$ _____

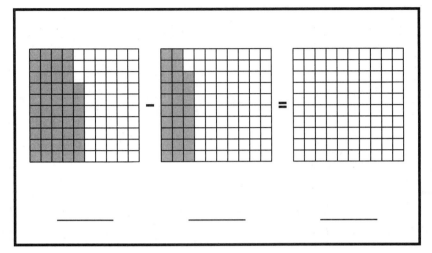

_____   _____   _____

Which statement is true about the product of $\frac{1}{3}$ and 9?

◯ The product is equal to one of the factors.

◯ The product is greater than both factors.

◯ The product is more than $\frac{1}{3}$ but less than 9.

◯ The product is less than both factors.

Write a story problem for the expression.

(5 + 8) – (3 + 5)

---

450 mL ◯ 4.5 L

If a cube has a side length of 5 inches, what is the volume of the cube?

$12\overline{)368}$

Nico bought his family 3 sub sandwiches to share. How much sandwich would each family member get if the subs were split evenly among the five of them?

A square unit is used to measure _____ and a cubic unit is used to measure _____.

$\frac{2}{3}$ ◯ $\frac{8}{12}$

Asher had $\frac{3}{4}$ bag of peanuts. His brother ate $\frac{1}{2}$ of his peanuts. What fraction of the whole bag did Asher's brother eat?

Circle the largest number. Underline the smallest number.

607.3, 607.33, 607.333,

607.03, 607.033

Write an expression.
**subtract five from fifty,
then divide by 9**

Angel must have $\frac{1}{2}$ of her science project completed by next week. She finished $\frac{1}{4}$ of it last week and $\frac{1}{5}$ last night. How much more does she need to complete to meet the deadline of $\frac{1}{2}$ complete? Show your work.

What is the volume of the cube shown below?

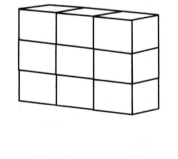

78.6 $\bigcirc$ 78.599

$$\begin{array}{r} 898.98 \\ +\ 77.07 \\ \hline \end{array}$$

Quarts	Gallons
	1
12	
	5
24	
	10

$$\begin{array}{r} 54 \\ \times\ 36 \\ \hline \end{array}$$

The area of a rectangle is 12 square inches. If the length is 4 inches, what is the width?

$4\frac{4}{5} \times \frac{1}{5} =$ _____

425
× 72

48.90, 48.94, 48.98, 49.02, . . .

Rule _____

Circle the quadrilaterals that are rectangles.

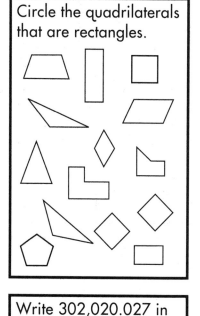

$\times \frac{1}{2}$

10 ⇒ _____

8 ⇒ _____

14 ⇒ _____

2 ⇒ _____

6 ⇒ _____

12 ⇒ _____

20 ⇒ _____

3 ⇒ _____

The blocks below are stacked from heaviest (bottom) to lightest (top). All of the labels fell off when they were stacked. Write the correct label on each block.

$\frac{3}{4}$ kg   0.50 kg $\frac{7}{10}$ kg $\frac{10}{20}$ kg

0.70 kg $\frac{4}{5}$ kg   0.75 kg   0.80 kg

_____	_____
_____	_____
_____	_____
_____	_____

Write 302,020.027 in word form.

$528,092 \div 10^3 =$ _____

$4 \times$ ⭐ $= 44$

$44 \div 4 =$ ⭐

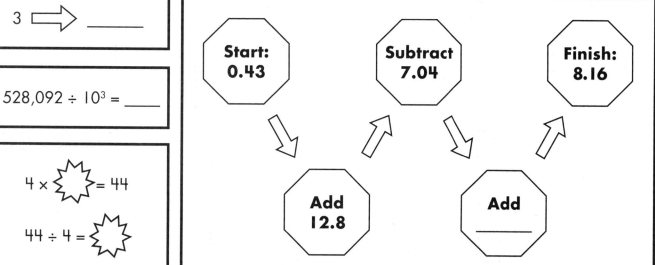

Start: 0.43

Subtract 7.04

Finish: 8.16

Add 12.8

Add _____

Find the product using the area model.

$\frac{1}{4} \times \frac{1}{5} =$ _____

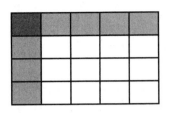

Solve. What patterns do you see?

35 ÷ 5 = _____	44 ÷ 4 = _____
350 ÷ 5 = ___	440 ÷ 4 = ____
3,500 ÷ 5 = ___	4,400 ÷ 4 = ___
72 ÷ 6 = _____	108 ÷ 12 = _____
720 ÷ 6 = _____	1,080 ÷ 12 = ____
7,200 ÷ 6 = _____	10,800 ÷ 12 = ___

611.2
× 7.2

Round the answer to the nearest

thousand

_____

hundred

_____

ten

_____

tenth

_____

Rule: Multiply by $\frac{1}{2}$

In	Out
8	
4	2
16	
32	

1.8
× 8

What is the value of the 1 in 2,637,134.25?

Kathleen purchased 4 yards of ribbon. She uses $\frac{1}{3}$ yard to make a bow. How many bows can she make in all?

Plot the points on the coordinate plane.

(3, 0)   (1, 1)
(4, 4)   (2, 5)

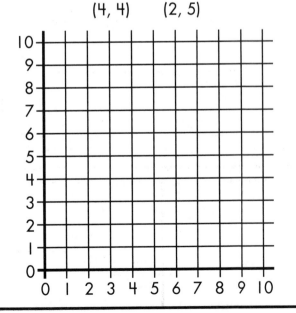

$7,800 \div 10^4 =$ _____

Solve for z. Show your work.

7 × (9 − z) = 21

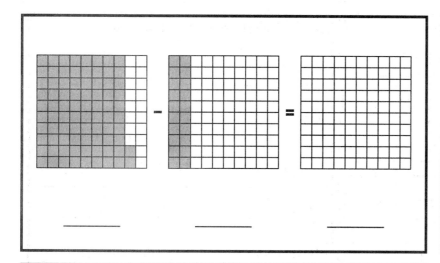

_____   _____   _____

400,000 = 40 _____

○ thousands

○ hundred thousands

○ ten thousands

○ millions

Which has more volume? How do you know?

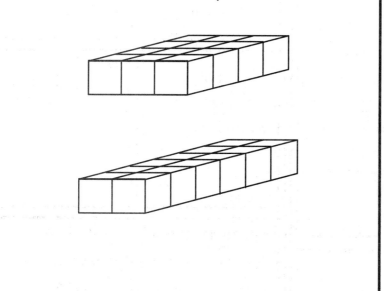

4 cups = _____ fluid ounces

Use the geoboard to show $\frac{1}{8} \times \frac{1}{2}$.

$\frac{99}{100}$ is closer to which benchmark number? Color your answer.

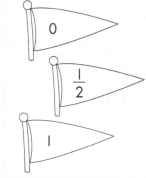

0

$\frac{1}{2}$

1

Place each fraction on the number line. Then, round to the nearest whole number.

| | | |
11   12   13

A. $\frac{23}{2}$ _____   B. $\frac{37}{3}$ _____   C. $\frac{47}{4}$ _____   D. $\frac{64}{5}$ _____

Write as a decimal.

$(9 \times 100) + (7 \times 10) + (1 \times \frac{1}{10}) + (8 \times \frac{1}{100})$

$10 \times \frac{1}{5} =$ _____

Which product will have 4 decimal places?

○ 3.5 × 8.1   ○ 4.84 × 0.1

○ 8.54 × 0.13   ○ 0.12 × 8.3

Which number is equivalent to
$0.068 × 10^4$?

○ 68   ○ 0.68

○ 680   ○ 6,800

I mile is _____ times as long as
I foot.

JP is making trail mix with the recipe below. He then
plans to package the trail mix in bags in 1-cup servings.
How many bags can JP make?

Trail Mix
$1\frac{2}{3}$ cup raisins
2 cup peanuts
$\frac{1}{2}$ cup chocolate chips
$1\frac{3}{4}$ cup dried pineapple

What is the volume of this object?

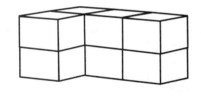

67.8 ◯ 67.08

2,100.07
− 383.28

Which of the following
equations could be used
to find the volume of the
prism?

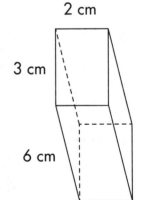

2 cm

3 cm

6 cm

○ V = 6 + (2 + 3)
○ V = 3 × 2 × 6
○ V = 3 + 2 × 6
○ V = (2 × 3) + (3 × 6)

21
× 18

Estimate the product of 34.5 × 3.1.

$1\frac{4}{5} \times 1\frac{1}{5} =$ _____

302
× 23

$\frac{4}{7}$ ◯ 0.500

What is the name of the angle that measures exactly 90°?

Draw an example.

Color all fractions equivalent to 1.

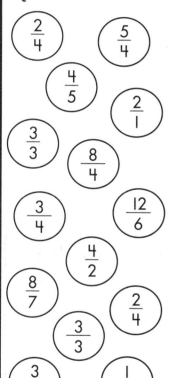

$\frac{2}{4}$ $\frac{5}{4}$

$\frac{4}{5}$

$\frac{2}{1}$

$\frac{3}{3}$ $\frac{8}{4}$

$\frac{3}{4}$ $\frac{12}{6}$

$\frac{4}{2}$

$\frac{8}{7}$ $\frac{2}{4}$

$\frac{3}{3}$

$\frac{3}{2}$ $\frac{1}{7}$

Write a story problem for the expression $(8 + 4) \div 3$.

Write as a decimal.

one and three thousandths

$400.05 \times 10^3 =$ _____

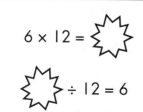

$6 \times 12 =$ ⬟

⬟ $\div 12 = 6$

Color the petals on each flower that are factors of the center number.

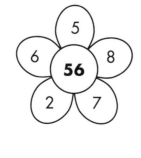

5
6   56   8
2   7

3
4   72   5
6   8

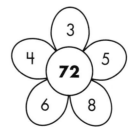

5
7   45   2
9   3

Name _____ **Week 36, Day 2**

Find the product using the area model.

$$\frac{3}{4} \times \frac{2}{3} = \underline{\hspace{1cm}}$$

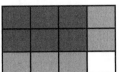

Find the area.

$4\frac{1}{4}$ yd.

$6\frac{2}{3}$ yd.

Rule: +4	Rule: +1	Ordered Pair
0	0	(0, 0)

What time will it be in $4\frac{1}{4}$ hours?

_____

6.2
× 8

Fill in the missing number.

$\boxed{}$

– 8.6
1.8

Each weekday, Nolan is in school for 6.5 hours. How many total minutes does Nolan attend school each week?

Total seconds?

Three-fourths of a pizza is left. Four friends want to share the leftovers equally. What part of the whole pizza will each friend get?

Rule: Divide by 10

_____, 30,400, _____, _____, _____

$$3 \div \frac{1}{2} = \underline{\hspace{1cm}}$$

158 © Carson-Dellosa • CD-104885

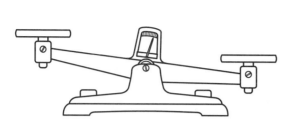

Write one of the measurements on each side to make the scale true.

14,200 pounds   7 tons

Six hundred forty-two and three hundred five thousandths can also be written as

○ 642,305.

○ 642.035.

○ 642.305.

○ 642.350.

Write a story problem for the expression (49 − 4) ÷ 5.

---

10 yards ◯ 380 inches

Cherisse ran $\frac{2}{3}$ the way around the track and stopped. If she did this 4 more times, how many laps did she run in all?

$13\overline{)9,412}$

Eli and his three brothers planned to share the three leftover brownies. How much brownie would they each get if they shared fairly?
Show your work.

Write as a decimal.

fourteen thousand and twenty hundredths

$\frac{4}{5}$ ◯ $\frac{3}{7}$

Which of the following is equal to eleven thousand five and two hundredths?

○ 11,000.52   ○ 11,005.02

○ 11,050.02   ○ 11,005.2

Circle the largest number. Underline the smallest number.

44.54, 45.44, 54.32, 54.48, 44.99

Write the expression.
eight less than the product of twelve and 5

In January, the class was $\frac{1}{2}$ way to meeting their reading goal. In March, they were $\frac{1}{3}$ closer. How much more do they need to meet their goal? Show your work.

What is the volume of this object?

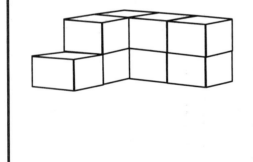

78.076 ○ 78.09

500.45 – 488.5

301
× 12

If the length of a rectangular rug is $8\frac{1}{3}$ feet and the width is 9 feet, what is the area of the rug? Show your work.

Pints	Quarts
2	
4	
	8
	9
20	

$\frac{4}{5} \times \frac{6}{7} =$ _____

$$\begin{array}{r} 4.8 \\ \underline{\times\ 0.5} \end{array}$$

100.25, 100.50, 100.75, 101.00, . . .

Rule _____

Draw a trapezoid.

List the properties.
Sides:
Vertices:
Other:

Round each number to the place of the underlined digit.

60.956 _____

5,555.55 _____

78.904 _____

39.248 _____

5.987 _____

The blocks below are stacked from heaviest (bottom) to lightest (top). All of the labels fell off when they were stacked. Write the correct label on each block.

| $\frac{4}{4}$ kg | 0.5 kg | 5 kg | $\frac{500}{1000}$ kg |

| 1 kg | $\frac{2}{5}$ kg | $\frac{5}{1}$ kg | 0.4 kg |

Write 777.200 in word form.

$4,000 \times 10^3 =$ _____

☆ × 9 = 108

108 ÷ 9 = ☆

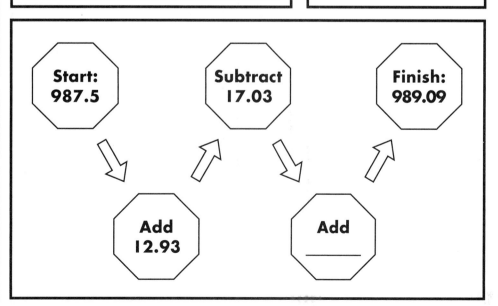

Start: 987.5

Add 12.93

Subtract 17.03

Add _____

Finish: 989.09

Use the area model to find the product.

$$\frac{5}{6} \times \frac{2}{3} = \underline{\hspace{1cm}}$$

45.82
× 6.4

Round the answer to the nearest

hundred.

_____

ten.

_____

tenth.

_____

hundredth.

_____

Rule: Multiply by $\frac{3}{4}$

In	Out
4	3
8	6
12	
16	

Solve. What patterns do you see?

8 × 3 = _____	12 × 8 = _____
80 × 30 = _____	120 × 8 = _____
800 × 300 = _____	1,200 × 8 = _____
5 × 6 = _____	11 × 5 = _____
50 × 6 = _____	110 × 5 = _____
500 × 6 = _____	1,100 × 5 = _____

12
× 2.3

What is the value of the 7 in 278,361.803?

Identify the points on the graph.

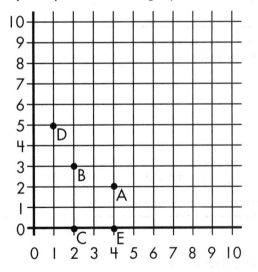

A _____   B _____   C _____

D _____   E _____

For the family reunion, Thomas made $\frac{1}{2}$ gallon of lemonade for his cousins. If he pours all of the lemonade into 8 cups equally, how much lemonade does each cousin get?

$$3.401 \times 10^4 =$$

Solve for *m*. Show your work.

$$4 \times (m \div 3) = 16$$

If Catherine measured the volume of a large box, which of the following could be her results?

○ 7.5 cubic yards

○ 7.5 square yards

○ 7.5 yards

○ 7.5 pounds

What is $\frac{6}{8}$ in simplest form?

○ $\frac{1}{4}$　　　○ $\frac{2}{3}$

○ $\frac{3}{16}$　　　○ $\frac{3}{4}$

The rectangular prism has a volume of 48 cubic inches. Find the missing measurement.

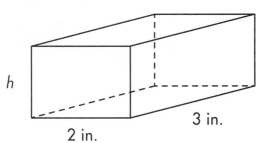

h

2 in.

3 in.

$h =$ _____

7 pints = _____ cups

Use the geoboard to show $\frac{3}{16} + \frac{3}{16} + \frac{5}{8}$.

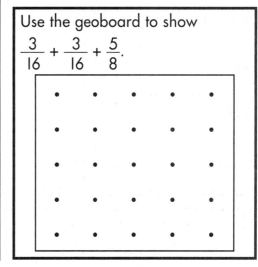

$\frac{6}{20}$ is closer to which benchmark number? Color your answer.

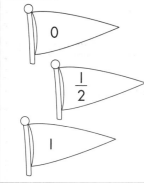

0

$\frac{1}{2}$

1

Place each number on the number line. Then, round to the nearest whole number.

48　　　　　　　　　　　　　　　　　　　　　49

A. 48.020 _____　B. $48\frac{20}{100}$ _____　C. 48.750 _____　D. $48\frac{1}{3}$ _____

Write as a decimal.

thirteen and four hundredths

$8 \times \frac{3}{4} =$ _____

Which product will have five decimal places?

◯ 7.1 × 8.43   ◯ 2.377 × 4.1

◯ 0.544 × 0.94   ◯ 2 × 9.246

Which number is equivalent to
$423 ÷ 10^3$?

◯ 4.23   ◯ 0.423

◯ 4,230   ◯ 42.3

I _____ is 100,000 times as long as 1 centimeter.

On Monday, Whitney was able to swim $\frac{1}{3}$ the length of the pool without stopping. At Tuesday's practice, she made it $\frac{3}{4}$ of the way without stopping. How much farther did she swim on Tuesday? Show your work.

What is the volume of this object?

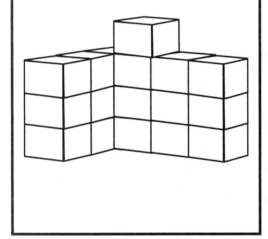

809.22 ◯ 809.301

214.57
− 120.28

$6\frac{1}{3}$ mi.

$2\frac{1}{2}$ mi.

Perimeter _____

Area _____

50
× 75

Rita bought a 12-ounce box of pasta for $1.80. How much did she spend on each ounce?

$1\frac{1}{2} \times 1\frac{1}{3} =$ _____

$$918 \\ \times\ 55$$

$\frac{7}{9}$ ◯ $\frac{2}{3}$

Polygon name:

_____

Number of sides: _____

Number of parallel sides: _____

Number of right angles:

_____

Color all fractions equivalent to $\frac{1}{2}$ but less than 1.

$\frac{3}{4}$ $\frac{5}{5}$ $\frac{2}{5}$ $\frac{3}{5}$ $\frac{2}{6}$ $\frac{2}{3}$ $\frac{4}{9}$ $\frac{1}{3}$ $\frac{4}{6}$ $\frac{7}{8}$ $\frac{5}{7}$ $\frac{5}{4}$ $\frac{3}{2}$ $\frac{3}{7}$

Color the path of equivalence from start to finish without diagonal movement.

Start: $\frac{1}{6}$	$\frac{7}{42}$	$\frac{3}{18}$
$\frac{2}{3}$	$\frac{8}{9}$	$\frac{3}{48}$
$\frac{17}{20}$	$\frac{5}{30}$	$\frac{2}{12}$
0.6	$\frac{10}{60}$	$\frac{8}{10}$
$\frac{4}{5}$	$\frac{11}{66}$	Finish!

Write as a decimal.

seventeen and eighty-nine thousandths

$837.47 \times 10^3 =$ _____

$3 \times$ ✦ $= 24$

$24 \div 3 =$ ✦

Color the petals on each flower that are factors of the center number.

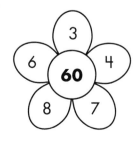

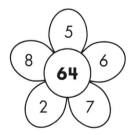

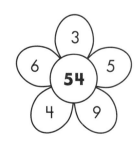

Use the area model to find the product.

$$\frac{3}{4} \times \frac{1}{2} = \underline{\hspace{1cm}}$$

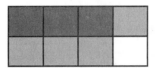

Find the area.

$14\frac{1}{3}$ mi.

8 mi.

Rule: +5	Rule: +4	Ordered Pair
0	0	(0, 0)

$0.12\overline{)24.48}$

9.81 × 7

Fill in the missing number.

$$\boxed{}$$
$$- \ 0.4$$
$$\overline{0.2}$$

Andee is learning to play the piano. Her instructor said she needs 10 hours of practice before her next recital. Plot her data on a line plot. Has Andee practiced enough for her recital? Explain how you know.

Week 1	Week 2	Week 3	Week 4
$1\frac{3}{4}$ hours	$1\frac{1}{8}$ hours	$1\frac{1}{8}$ hours	$1\frac{3}{4}$ hours

Week 5	Week 6	Week 7
$1\frac{3}{8}$ hours	$1\frac{5}{8}$ hours	$1\frac{3}{4}$ hours

The chocolate chip cookie recipe called for $\frac{1}{2}$ cup of chocolate chips per dozen. How many dozen cookies can you make with 3 cups of chocolate chips?

Rule: Multiply by 10

_____, 34.56, _____, _____, _____

$$\frac{1}{4} \div 2 = \underline{\hspace{1cm}}$$

Name _____   **Week 38, Day 3**

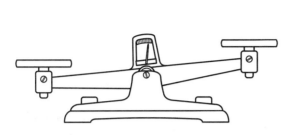

Write one of the measurements on each side to make the scale true.

20,000 kg   19.5 kg

What is 102.38 ÷ 10?

○ 10.238

○ 102.38

○ 1023.8

○ 1.0238

Write a story problem for the expression (8 + 4) ÷ 3.

---

5 hr. ◯ 360 min.

Use order of operations to solve. Show your work for each step.

4 × (7 + 3) ÷ 4 – 5

---

17)3,162

A class of 18 students shared a dozen doughnuts fairly. How much doughnut did each student receive? Show your work.

Write as a decimal.

six hundred forty-two and seven thousandths

$20 ÷ \frac{1}{4}$

Which product will have 4 decimal places?

◯ 3.1 × 7.9   ◯ 6.38 × 0.9

◯ 1.2 × 1.83   ◯ 3 × 5.932

Which number is equivalent to
9.76×10^3?

◯ 97.6   ◯ 9,760

◯ 976   ◯ 0.976

Write an expression.
**add 6 and 7, then multiply
by 3**

Frances made $17\frac{3}{4}$ cups of tea for the reunion. There
were $4\frac{1}{2}$ cups left after the reunion. How much tea did
they drink at the reunion?

What is the volume of this object?

78.708 ◯ 78.8

$742.63
+ $98.99

Feet	Yards
	3
	5
	7
	8
	10

13
× 42

Adrian earns $6.50 an hour
babysitting. If he babysat twelve
hours last week, how much money
did he earn?

$2\frac{3}{4} \times 2\frac{1}{2} =$ _____

Fill in the missing number.

$$\boxed{}$$
$$\underline{-\ 2.1}$$
$$3.17$$

$\frac{1}{6}, \frac{1}{2}, \frac{5}{6}, \frac{7}{6}, \cdots$

Rule _____

Polygon name:

_____

Number of sides: _____

Number of parallel
sides: _____

Number of right angles:

_____

Round each number to the place of the underlined digit.

78.5<u>5</u>3 _____

8,9<u>2</u>6.4 _____

908.<u>2</u>3 _____

8<u>7</u>.567 _____

83.2<u>8</u>9 _____

The blocks below are stacked from heaviest (bottom) to lightest (top). All of the labels fell off when they were stacked. Write the correct label on each block.

$\frac{4}{2}$ kg $\frac{3}{5}$ kg   2.5 kg $\frac{250}{100}$ kg

$\frac{4}{16}$ kg   0.6 kg   2 kg $\frac{250}{1000}$ kg

_____	_____
_____	_____
_____	_____
_____	_____

Write 222,050.038 in word form.

$0.7 \div 10^2 =$ _____

$8 \times 12 = $ ☆

☆ $\div 12 = 8$

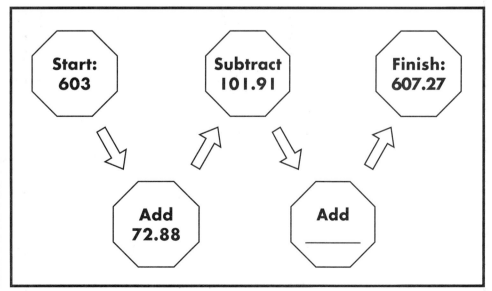

Start: 603   **Subtract 101.91**   **Finish: 607.27**

Add 72.88   **Add** _____

Use the area model to find the product.

$\frac{1}{8} \times \frac{3}{4} =$ _____

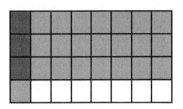

77.09

× 3.8

Round the answer to the nearest

hundred

_____

ten

_____

tenth

_____

hundredth

_____

Rule: Multiply by $\frac{2}{3}$

In	Out
3	2
9	
18	
12	

Solve. What patterns do you see?

24 ÷ 8 = _____	96 ÷ 12 = _____
240 ÷ 8 = _____	960 ÷ 12 = _____
2,400 ÷ 8 = _____	9,600 ÷ 12 = _____
30 ÷ 6 = _____	55 ÷ 5 = _____
300 ÷ 6 = _____	550 ÷ 5 = _____
3,000 ÷ 6 = _____	5,500 ÷ 5 = _____

8.88

×   8

What is the value of the 8 in 1,700,023.801?

The 4-person relay team will run a total of 5 miles. How much will each member run if they each run the same distance?

$33,000 \div 10^5 =$ _____

Solve for a. Show your work.

$$3 \times [2 \times (a - 16)] = 42$$

Identify the points on the graph.

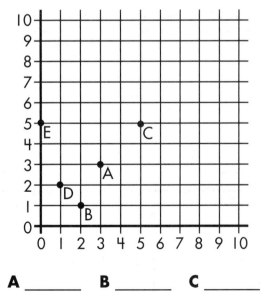

A _____   B _____   C _____

D _____   E _____

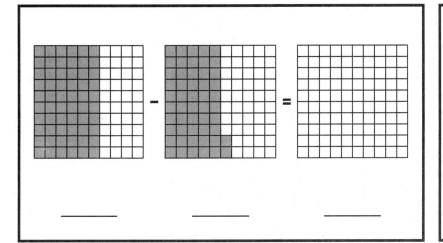

_____ _____ _____

Which of the following is a composite number?

◯ 7

◯ 13

◯ 19

◯ 21

Griff has an L-shaped terrarium. Which expression can be used to find the volume of Griff's terrarium?

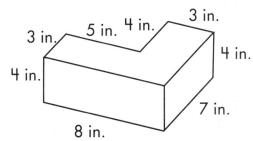

◯ (8 × 4 × 7) + (4 × 4 × 5)

◯ (4 × 4 × 8) + (3 × 4 × 5)

◯ (8 × 4 × 3) + (4 × 4 × 3)

◯ (3 × 4 × 7) + (8 × 5 × 3)

3 gallons 9 cups = _____ cups

Use the geoboard to show $\frac{1}{2} \times \frac{1}{4}$.

$\frac{10}{90}$ is closer to which benchmark number? Color your answer.

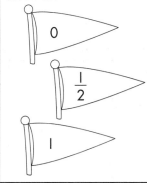

0

$\frac{1}{2}$

1

Place each number on the number line. Then, round to the nearest whole number.

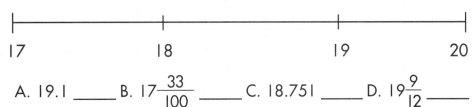

17   18   19   20

A. 19.1 _____ B. $17\frac{33}{100}$ _____ C. 18.751 _____ D. $19\frac{9}{12}$ _____

Write as a decimal.

(6 × 100) + (7 × 10) + (2 × $\frac{1}{100}$) + (1 × $\frac{1}{1,000}$)

$\frac{5}{6} \times 12 =$ _____

Circle the largest number. Underline the smallest number.

81.1, 81.01, 81.11, 81.001, 81.111

Jack's company has a total of $1,000 to give to its employees as a bonus. Write an expression to represent how much money each employee would get if the money is divided equally among the employees. Let *e* represent employees. Show your work.

1 kilometer is 1,000,000 times as long as 1 _____.

Jackie lives $3\frac{3}{8}$ miles from the library. Kate lives $2\frac{1}{4}$ miles from the library.

Who lives closer to the library? _____

How much closer? _____

What is the volume of this object?

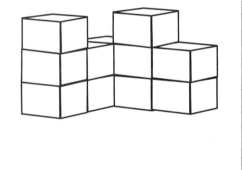

6,725.725 ◯ 6,725.9

651.10
− 562.25

Pounds	Ounces
1	
2	
3	
6	
	160

55
× 19

Taylor's rectangular backyard measures 18 feet by 22 feet. What is the total area of her backyard?

Name _____

$6\frac{1}{2} \times \frac{3}{4} =$ _____

Fill in the missing number.

$- 3.3$

0.09

$0.01 \bigcirc \frac{1}{10}$

Polygon name:
_____

Number of sides: _____

Number of parallel sides: _____

Number of right angles: _____

Color all fractions equivalent to $\frac{1}{2}$.

$\frac{1}{6}$ $\frac{5}{6}$

$\frac{2}{4}$ $\frac{1}{4}$

$\frac{3}{4}$ $\frac{3}{7}$

$\frac{5}{8}$ $\frac{3}{9}$

$\frac{4}{7}$

$\frac{9}{10}$ $\frac{7}{10}$

$\frac{1}{3}$

$\frac{1}{5}$ $\frac{4}{7}$

Color the path of equivalence from start to finish without diagonal movement..

Start: $\frac{12}{32}$	$\frac{1}{4}$	$\frac{16}{20}$
$\frac{6}{16}$	$\frac{15}{40}$	$\frac{14}{18}$
0.6	$\frac{3}{8}$	$\frac{9}{20}$
$\frac{12}{20}$	$\frac{18}{48}$	$\frac{9}{24}$
$\frac{1}{6}$	$\frac{4}{24}$	Finish!

Write as a decimal.

five thousand forty-two and thirty-five thousandths

$0.67 \times 10^5 =$ _____

$5 \times \text{☆} = 30$

$30 \div 5 = \text{☆}$

Color the petals on each flower that are factors of the center number.

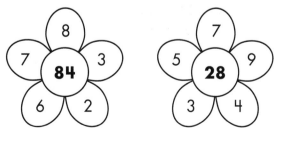

How many thousandths are equivalent to
6 hundredths?

◯ 6   ◯ 6,000

◯ 60   ◯ 600

Find the area.

$3\frac{3}{4}$ ft.

$2\frac{1}{2}$ ft.

Rule: +6	Rule: +4	Ordered Pair
0	0	(0, 0)

What time will it be in
$2\frac{3}{4}$ hours?

_____

$$\begin{array}{r} 7.63 \\ \times\quad 9 \\ \hline \end{array}$$

Fill in the missing number.

$$\begin{array}{r} \boxed{} \\ -\ 5.3 \\ \hline 4.8 \end{array}$$

Find the product. Show your work.

$$\frac{7}{10} \times \frac{2}{3}$$

Fill in the blanks to complete the area model
showing 184 × 18.

	100	80	4
10	1,000	___	40
8	___	640	32

$$\begin{array}{r} 1,000 \\ \underline{} \\ \underline{} \\ 640 \\ 40 \\ +\quad 32 \\ \hline \underline{} \end{array}$$

Rule: Divide by 10

_____, 99,000, _____, _____, _____

$2 \div \dfrac{1}{3} = $ _____

A pitcher contained $1\frac{3}{4}$ liters of lemonade. The friends drank $\frac{2}{3}$ of the lemonade at lunch. How much lemonade is left in the pitcher? Show your work.

12 − (3 + 5)

○ 13

○ 4

○ 20

○ 5

Write a story problem for the expression 3 × (4 + 2).

400 cm ◯ 3.75 m

Tony skied down a hill that was 4 miles long. Flags were placed at every $\frac{1}{4}$ of a mile. How many flags were there in all?

$16\overline{)1{,}248}$

The children's museum is open 8 hours a day. Each day, they have 12 tours scheduled. How long does each tour last? Show your work.

Write as a decimal.

eighty-one and five hundredths

$\frac{1}{8} \div 2$

Which product will have 4 decimal places?

○ 3.22 × 8.5   ○ 7.3 × 0.33

○ 0.5 × 0.94   ○ 2.111 × 7.2

Which number is equivalent to $987.2 \div 10^2$?

○ 9.872   ○ 98.72

○ 9,872   ○ 987.02

Write an expression.
the product of 7 and a number decreased by 5

Miguel practiced piano for $\frac{3}{4}$ hours on Thursday and $\frac{2}{3}$ hours on Saturday. How many total hours did Miguel practice?

What is the volume of this object?

506.009 ◯ 506.01

908.03
− 473.57

Pounds	Tons
6,000	
10,000	
	7
	9
	10

66
× 44

Since 5 divided by $\frac{1}{5}$ = 25, then $25 \times \frac{1}{5}$ = _____.

$3\frac{1}{3} \times 1\frac{7}{9} =$

$4 \div \frac{1}{2} =$

$\frac{1}{3} \div 9 =$

$\frac{1}{2} \div 12 =$

$2\frac{6}{11} \times 5\frac{1}{2} =$

$10 \div \frac{3}{4} =$

$\frac{6}{7} \div 4 =$

$\frac{3}{8} \div 3 =$

$\frac{1}{8} \times \frac{1}{7} =$

$6 \div \frac{2}{3} =$

$3 \div \frac{5}{8} =$

$\frac{3}{4} \div 4 =$

$\frac{3}{7} \times \frac{1}{10} =$

$8 \div \frac{1}{4} =$

$5 \div \frac{3}{5} =$

$\frac{2}{5} \div 10 =$

$5\frac{25}{27}$	8	$\frac{1}{27}$	$\frac{1}{24}$
14	$13\frac{1}{3}$	$\frac{3}{14}$	$\frac{1}{8}$
$\frac{1}{56}$	9	$4\frac{4}{5}$	$\frac{3}{16}$
$\frac{3}{70}$	32	$8\frac{1}{3}$	$\frac{1}{25}$

$$6\frac{2}{5}$$
$$+\ 4\frac{2}{3}$$

$$5\frac{1}{6}$$
$$+\ 7\frac{8}{9}$$

$$\frac{2}{4}$$
$$+\ \frac{5}{7}$$

$$\frac{2}{12}$$
$$+\ \frac{3}{24}$$

$$4\frac{7}{8}$$
$$+\ 6\frac{3}{4}$$

$$2\frac{3}{8}$$
$$+\ 5\frac{1}{2}$$

$$\frac{3}{5}$$
$$+\ \frac{4}{7}$$

$$\frac{1}{6}$$
$$+\ \frac{1}{4}$$

$$5\frac{2}{5}$$
$$+\ 4\frac{3}{8}$$

$$4\frac{1}{2}$$
$$+\ 7\frac{3}{10}$$

$$11\frac{1}{3}$$
$$-\ 3\frac{2}{3}$$

$$\frac{11}{12}$$
$$-\ \frac{1}{6}$$

$$\frac{5}{7}$$
$$-\ \frac{2}{9}$$

$$8$$
$$-\ \frac{5}{8}$$

$$19$$
$$-\ \frac{1}{2}$$

$$8\frac{1}{2}$$
$$-\ 8\frac{1}{4}$$

$\dfrac{7}{24}$	$1\dfrac{3}{14}$	$13\dfrac{1}{18}$	$11\dfrac{1}{15}$
$\dfrac{5}{12}$	$1\dfrac{6}{35}$	$7\dfrac{7}{8}$	$11\dfrac{5}{8}$
$\dfrac{3}{4}$	$7\dfrac{2}{3}$	$11\dfrac{4}{5}$	$9\dfrac{31}{40}$
$\dfrac{1}{4}$	$18\dfrac{1}{2}$	$7\dfrac{3}{8}$	$\dfrac{31}{63}$

Answer Key

Day 1

Day 2

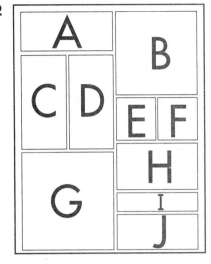

Day 3

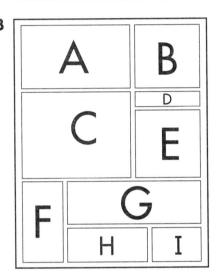

Day 4

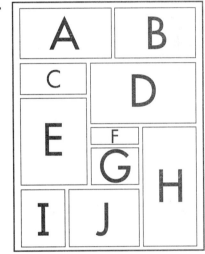

Week 1, Day 1 (page 17)
A. Check students' work. B. 487; C. +10; D. Check students' work. E. 6:12; F. Check students' work. rectangle; G. two and fifty-four hundredths; H. 21,000; I. 6, 7; J. Check students' work.

Week 1, Day 2 (page 18)
A. 594; B. 45, 450, 4,500; 12, 120, 1,200; 56, 560, 5,600; 12, 120, 1,200; C. Check students' work. D. 18.25; E. 318.56; F. 700; G. Check students' work. H. 8 × (430 + 44); I. 9, 12, 15; J. 28

Week 1, Day 3 (page 19)
A. 0.86 < 0.95; B. 12,287; C. seven hundred twenty-eight and twenty-nine hundredths, (7 × 100) + (2 × 10) + (8 × 1) + (2 × 1/10) + (9 × 1/100); D. 2,000; E. Check students' work. F. 4.23; G. Check students' work. 0, 1, 1, 0; H. 0.7; I. 777

Week 1, Day 4 (page 20)
A. 239; B. 5, 8, 11, 14, 17, 7, 12, 17, 22, 27; C. 60; D. 2 ones, 2 hundredths, 6 hundreds, 3 tenths, 1 thousandth; E. $8; F. <; G. 5,373; H. trapezoid, octagon, equilateral triangle, quadrilateral; I. 189; J. 21

Week 2, Day 1 (page 21)
A. 462; B. Line *AB*; C. >; D. pentagon; E. 0.5, 1.7, 3.5, 3.0, 0.7, 4.8, 7.9, 5.6; F. 3; G. 3.45; H. 45,000; I. 8, 56; J. 0.88, 0.61, 0.68, 0.7, 0.9

Week 2, Day 2 (page 22)
A. 19 in.; B. 1.98, 2.05, 2.12, 2.14; C. Yes, he has $3.62. D. (7, 42), (9, 54); E. 67.23; F. 1 1/4; G. (2, 2), (7, 4), (6, 8), (3, 7); H. $53; I. 100, 1,000, 10,000, 100,000; J. *m* × 3 = *n*

Answer Key

Week 2, Day 3 (page 23)
A. trapezoid, parallelogram; B. 34,885; C. three hundred fifteen and eighty-nine hundredths, $(3 \times 100) + (1 \times 10) + (5 \times 1) + (8 \times 1/10) + (9 \times 1/100)$; D.<; E. 35, 42, 21, 56, 14; F. 3,346.2, 3,300; G. 5, 4, 4, 7, 10, 12, 9; H. 7.86, 7.9, 8; I. 234,589

Week 2, Day 4 (page 24)
A. 3.4; B. m, mm, km, m, cm; C. $b + 15$; D. 5/8; E. 7.7; F. <; G. $8.02; H. isosceles; I. 42.69; J. 24

Week 3, Day 1 (page 25)
A. Check students' work. B. 5/8, 4/6, 2/4, 2/10; C. add 4; D. pentagon, hexagon, right triangle, rhombus; E. 11, 19, 5; F. Check students' work. G. thirty-two and eighty-one hundredths; H. 15,000; I. 8, 4; J. 22.7

Week 3, Day 2 (page 26)
A. 2; B. 9, 90, 900; 3, 30, 300; 7, 70, 700; 6, 60, 600; C. 1/2, 0.5; D. 4:45; E. 469.67; F. 2,000; G. Check students' work. H. 2.88 = 2.8; I. 15, 20, 25; J. 33

Week 3, Day 3 (page 27)
A. Check students' work. B. 0.528; C. eight hundred twenty and eight hundredths, $(8 \times 100) + (2 \times 10) + (8 \times 1/100)$; D. 12; E–F. Check students' work. G. 1, 1, 1, 0; H. 0.19; I. 1

Week 3, Day 4 (page 28)
A. 3; B. 28, 49; C. liter; D.108 sq. m; E. divide 65 by 5, then subtract 4; F. <; G. 23,381; H. 36 cm, 77 sq. cm; I. 91; J. origin

Week 4, Day 1 (page 29)
A. Check students' work. Because they intersect at 90°. B. 1, 2, 3, 4, 6, 8, 12, 24; 2 and 3 circled; C. <; D. Check students' work. 4, 4, opposites sides are congruent, opposite angles are congruent, and opposite sides are parallel; E. 1.0, 3.7, 2.8, 1.4, 2.0, 4.6, 5.8, 3.3; F. 11; G. 5.016; H. 16,000; I. 3, 3; J. 10.3

Week 4, Day 2 (page 30)
A. $b - 6 = p$; B. $(19 - 5) \div 2$; $(25 + 8) \times 3$; C. 23,849, 20,000, 24,000, 23,800, 23,850; D. No, she has $29.98. E. 68.65; F. 6.6; G. (2, 4), (3, 7), (7, 9), (5, 4), (7, 6); H. 0.05; I. 1,000, 100, 10, 1; J. 5, 21, 10

Week 4, Day 3 (page 31)
A. >; B. 5.672; C. seven hundred four and four hundredths, $(7 \times 100) + (4 \times 1) + (4 \times 1/100)$; D. = ; E. 54, 27, 72, 81, 45, 36; F. 1/2; G. 1/3; H. 18.45, 18.5, 18; I. <

Week 4, Day 4 (page 32)
A. $(1 \times 10) + (5 \times 1) + (3 \times 1/10) + (8 \times 1/100)$; B. addition; C. $21 - n$; D. 5/8; E. 0.57; F. <; G. 546; H. 30 in., 54 sq. in; I. 1, 2, 3, 4, 6, 9, 12, 18, 36; J. 1 2/5

Week 5, Day 1 (page 33)
A. Check students' work. B. 6.02; C. add 9; D. acute angle; E. 345, 4,670.5, 280, 892.3, 106; F. Check students' work. G. two hundred ninety-one and thirty-two hundredths; H. 7,200; I. 18, 9; J. 10.7

Week 5, Day 2 (page 34)
A. 15.746; B. 42, 420, 4,200; 36, 360, 3,600; 32, 320, 3,200; 18, 180, 1,800; C. 1/4, 0.25; D. 7:45; E. 1,320.39; F. 4,000; G. Check students' work. H. 2/3 and 4/6; I. 6, 10, 14, 18; J. 3

Week 5, Day 3 (page 35)
A. Check students' work. B. twenty-one and fourteen thousandths; C. sixty-three and twenty-seven hundredths, $(6 \times 10) + (3 \times 1) + (2 \times 1/10) + (7 \times 1/100)$; D. 3,000; E. Check students' work. F. 99; G. Check students' work. 0, 2, 1, 1; H. 0.53; I. <

Week 5, Day 4 (page 36)
A. $(7 \times 10) + (8 \times 1) + (1 \times 1/10) + (6 \times 1/100)$; B. multiplication; C. two; D. 3.5, 6.13, no; E. 0.89; F. >; G. 395; H. 40 ft., 75 sq. ft.; I. 1, 2, 3, 6, 7, 14, 21, 42; J. $3.87

Week 6, Day 1 (page 37)
A. 50°; B. 139.86; C. <; D. Check students' work. E. 1.8, 3.3, 4.1, 1.9, 6.5, 4.0, 7.4, 4.6; F. 9 mi.; G. 4.019; H. 98,000; I. 9, 3; J. 0.5, 0.46, 0.7, 0.9, 0.6, 0.62, 0.49

Answer Key

Week 6, Day 2 (page 38)
A. 7; B. 2 × (6 − 2) ÷ 2; C. 48,280, 50,000, 48,000, 48,300, 48,280; D. Tommy, Answers will vary. E. 339.31; F. 5.5; G. Check students' work. H. 4/16 and 1/4; I. 120, 1,200, 12,000, 120,000; J. (4 × 1) + (9 × 1/10) + (3 × 1/100)

Week 6, Day 3 (page 39)
A. >; B. 416.305; C. forty-two and seven hundred eighty-nine thousandths, (4 × 10) + (2 × 1) + (7 × 1/10) + (8 × 1/100) + (9 × 1/1,000), 4, 2, 7, 8, 9; D. >; E. 32, 24, 48, 8, 64, 72; F. 1/2; G. 0.74 > 0.45; H. 27.21, 27.2, 27; I. =

Week 6, Day 4 (page 40)
A. 505,000.029; B. largest: 54.48, smallest: 44.54; C. 9 + x; D. 1 1/2 miles; E. 0.31; F. <; G. 243.99; H. 1,000, 3, 5,000, 7, 12; I. 350; J. 40 min., Answers will vary.

Week 7, Day 1 (page 41)
A. arrow pointing to the left; B. 9/2 or 4 1/9; C. add 15; D. rhombus, Check students' work. E. 767, 400.3, 1,000, 34.8, 28.4; F. Check students' work. G. one thousand forty-two and thirty-eight hundredths; H. 4,874.9; I. 3, 7; J. 14.64

Week 7, Day 2 (page 42)
A. 8.9; B. 12, 120, 1,200; 7, 70, 700; 4, 40, 400; 9, 90, 900; C. 3/4, 0.75; D. 10:15; E. 42.12; F. 0.1; G. A (6, 2), B (1, 4), C (0, 5), D (8, 9), E (10, 0); H. 9/10 and 18/20; I. 9, 15, 21, 27; J. 17

Week 7, Day 3 (page 43)
A. Check students' work. B. 2,266; C. ten and one thousandth; 1, 0, 0, 0, 1; (1 × 10) + (1 × 1/1,000); D. 1; E. Check students' work. F. 551; G. Check students' work. 0, 1, 2, 1; H. 0.739; I. >

Week 7, Day 4 (page 44)
A.(9 × 10) + (3 × 1) + (4 × 1/100); B. subtraction; C. kilometer; D. 4.928, 4.99, 4.6, 5.2, 5.14; E. 0.64; F. <; G. 6,312; H. 50 ft., 144 sq. ft.; I. 200; J. 5 pizzas

Week 8, Day 1 (page 45)
A. 12 sq. ft.; B. 5.19; C. >; D. rectangle, square; E. 3.8, 5.6, 5.2, 11.0, 3.7, 9.4, 8.3, 6.1; F. Check students' work. H. 8.27; 395.2; I. 5, 5; J. 0.11, 0.09, 0.19, 0.20, 0.01, 0.1, 0.13

Week 8, Day 2 (page 46)
A. 80; B. 30,520; C. 2, 6, (2, 6); 3, 9, (3, 9); 4, 12, (4, 12); D. 75,339, 80,000, 75,000, 75,300, 75,340; E. 3,121.87; F. 17; G. from top to bottom, left to right: 9.5, 4.8, 4.7, 2.5, 2.3, 2.4, 1.3, 1.2, 1.1, 1.3; H. 5,577.09, 5,577.1, 5,577, 5,580, 5,600, 6,000; I. 50,000, 5,000, 500; J. thirty-eight and twenty-eight hundredths

Week 8, Day 3 (page 47)
A. 0.8 > 0.77; B. 13,000; C. fourteen and thirty-two thousandths, (1 × 10) + (4 × 1) + (3 × 1/100) + (2 × 1/1,000), 1, 4, 0, 3, 2; D. >; E. 72, 36, 96, 108, 84, 48; F. 1; G. 3/4 of an hour; H. 347.95, 347.9, 348; I. >

Week 8, Day 4 (page 48)
A. largest: 709.9, smallest: 709.700; B. 5 mm, 5 cm, 5 m, 5 km; C. x − 33; D. 2 1/3 cups; E. 0.4; F. <; G. 457.34; H. 2, 5,000, 9, 10,000, 15; I. 490; J. 192

Week 9, Day 1 (page 49)
A. 24 in.; B. 8/12, 2/3; C. add 12; D. D; E. 6.7, 4.8, 4.1, 8.8, 3, 5.3, 5.8, 4.2; F. 114 lb.; G. one hundred two and three hundredths; H. 31,478; I. 9, 72; J. 38.3

Week 9, Day 2 (page 50)
A. 13.5; B. 27, 270, 2,700; 72, 720, 7,200; 48, 480, 4,800; 24, 240, 2,400; C. 4/10, 0.4; D. 12:15; E. 388.85; F. 0.09; G. Check students' work. H. 18/27 and 2/3; I. 32, 28, 24, 20; J. 44

Week 9, Day 3 (page 51)
A. Check students' work. B. 69.51; C. eighteen and one hundred three thousandths; 1, 8, 1, 0, 3; (1 × 10) + (8 × 1) + (1 × 1/10) + (3 × 1/1,000); D. 3,000; E. Check students' work. F. 67 × 84; G. Check students' work. 6, 8, 8, 7; H. 4.059; I. >

Answer Key

Week 9, Day 4 (page 52)
A. (6 × 10) + (1 × 1) + (2 × 1/100) +
(4 × 1/1,000); B. subtraction; C. foot; D. 1 1/3;
E. 0.16; F. <; G. 25,973; H. 58 ft., 180 sq. ft.;
I. 450; J. 180

Week 10, Day 1 (page 53)
A. 9:07; B. 9.42; C. =; D. rectangle,
parallelogram; E. 3.5, 5.5, 4.7, 5.4, 4.5, 3.6,
6.5, 9; F. Check students' work. G. 0.13; H. 25;
I. 4, 4; J. 0.6, 0.5, 0.8, 0.42, 0.7, 0.900, 0.41

Week 10, Day 2 (page 54)
A. 500; B. $59,516; C. 4, 8, (4, 8); 6, 12,
(6, 12); 8, 16, (8, 16); D. 4,684; E. 11.43;
F. 3/4; G. 142 cups; H. 76.87; I. 32, 320,
3,200, 32,000; J. (8 × 100) + (7 × 10) + (3 × 1)
+ (1 × 1/10) + (7 × 1/00)

Week 10, Day 3 (page 55)
A. 0.6 = 0.60; B. 53.45; C. thirty-nine and two
hundred seventy-eight thousandths; 3, 9, 2, 7, 8;
(3 × 10) + (9 × 1) + (2 × 1/10) + (7 × 1/100) +
(8 × 1/1,000); D. >; E. 36, 12, 54, 24, 48, 42;
F. 714; G. H; H. 55.74, 55.7, 56; I. <

Week 10, Day 4 (page 56)
A. 468.19; B. 4 in., 4 ft., 4 yd., 4 mi.;
C. 126 – c; D. 5/6; E. 11 – (5 + 3) = 3,
(11 – 5) + 3 = 9; F. >; G. 31; H. 3, 7,000, 9,
5,000, 6; I. 154; J. 784.1, 7,841, 78,410,
784,100

Week 11, Day 1 (page 57)
A. Check students' work. B. 20; C. add 4;
D. B; E. 546.1, 9,820.05, 490, 1,003.0, 209;
F. Check students' work. rectangle; G. six
hundred seven and ten hundredths; H. 45; I. 4,
6; J. 25.2

Week 11, Day 2 (page 58)
A. 4.94; B. 3, 30, 300; 9, 90, 900; 12, 120,
1,200; 4, 40, 400; C. 1/2, 0.50; D. 5:30;
E. 526.26; F. seven tenths; G. Answers will vary.
H. 377.296; I. 77, 70, 63, 56; J. 18

Week 11, Day 3 (page 59)
A. 0.15 + 0.23 = 0.38; B. 12 c.; C. fifty-eight
and four hundred two thousandths, 5, 8, 4, 0, 2;
(5 × 10) + (8 × 1) + (4 × 1/10) + (2 × 1/1,000);
D. 2; E. Check students' work. F. 1; G. Check
students' work. 5, 4, 3, 4; H. 4.014; I. <

Week 11, Day 4 (page 60)
A. 780.73; B. 6.421; C. cm; D. Yes, she has 8 ft.
E. 1.58; F. =; G. 959.93; H. 90 ft., 450 sq. ft.;
I. 7,710; J. 6 hr.

Week 12, Day 1 (page 61)
A. Check students' work. B. 5/6; C. >;
D. rectangle, square, rhombus, parallelogram, 4
sides; E. 1.3, 3.4, 8.1, 3.7, 2.5, 6.0, 7.8, 8.9;
F. 1/2, 6/12, 2/4, 10/20, 30/60, 7/14, Finish;
G. 72.3; H. 3.645; I. 11, 77; J. 0.60, 0.400,
0.321, 0.670, 0.609, 0.008, 0.099, 0.6, 0.09

Week 12, Day 2 (page 62)
A. 20; B. 156; C. 1, 4, (1, 4); 2, 8, (2, 8);
3, 12, (3, 12); 4, 16, (4, 16); D. 26,708,
30,000, 27,000, 26,700, 26,710; E. 790.65;
F. 2.6; G. from top to bottom, left to right: 61.48,
24.71, 36.77, 12.14, 12.57, 24.2, 8.02, 4.12,
8.45, 15.75; H. 1,440, 10,080; I. 6,250, 625,
62.5, 6.25; J. (5 × 1,000) + (6 × 100) + (8 × 10)
+ (1 × 1) + (4 × 1/100)

Week 12, Day 3 (page 63)
A. 1,500 g, 1 kg; B. 48 in.; C. forty-three and
eight hundred sixty-two thousandths, 4, 3, 8, 6,
2; (4 × 10) + (3 × 1) + (8 × 1/10) + (6 × 1/100)
+ (2 × 1/1,000); D. <; E. associative; F. 907;
G. 0.59 < 0.79; H. 17.9, 18, 20; I. =

Week 12, Day 4 (page 64)
A. largest: 812.2, smallest: 811.897; B. 5 oz.,
5 lb., 5 T.; C. 174 – t; D. 7 5/8 yd.; E. 1.07;
F. >; G. 66 in.; H. 2, 5,000, 7,000, 3,000, 8; I.
3,588; J. 308

Week 13, Day 1 (page 65)
A. 90 in.; B. 2; C. multiply by 4; D. A; E. 514,
200, 251.0, 901.0, 405; F. $6.04; G. five and
six hundred seventy thousandths; H. 98.732;
I. 12, 12; J. 2.4

Answer Key

Week 13, Day 2 (page 66)
A. one thousand one hundred seventy-nine and three hundred sixty-three thousandths; B. 77, 770, 7,700; 60, 600, 6,000; 54, 540, 5,400; 64, 640, 6,400; C. 73/100, 0.73; D. 33,480, 30,000, 33,000, 33,500, 33,480; E. 139.93; F. 0.60; G. 10 mi.; H. $3.33; I. 36, 30, 24, 18; J. 18

Week 13, Day 3 (page 67)
A. 0.08 + 0.37 = 0.45; B. trapezoids; C. six and five thousandths, 6, 0, 0, 5; (6 × 1) + (5 × 1/1,000); D. 24; E. Check students' work. F. 0; G. Check students' work. 1, 3, 2, 3; H. 40.502; I. <

Week 13, Day 4 (page 68)
A. 6,030.603; B. 0.728; C. pound; D. 5/8; E. 432 in.; F. <; G. 6,470; H. 40 mi., 96 sq. mi.; I. 3,415; J. 300

Week 14, Day 1 (page 69)
A. 6 measuring cups; B. 9.54; C. >; D. square, rectangle, parallelogram, rhombus; E. 3.0, 5.2, 4.5, 4, 6.3, 9, 3.4, 7.9; F. 1/3, 3/9, 2/6, 10/30, 8/24, 5/15, Finish; G. 7,642.9; H. 78.92; I. 6, 6; J. 31.99, 32.200, 32.499, 32.5, 32.670, 32.098, 32.1, 32.111, 32.607

Week 14, Day 2 (page 70)
A. 345.6; B. $32.45; C. 2, 2, (2, 2); 4, 4, (4, 4); 6, 6, (6, 6); 8, 8, (8, 8); D. 12:40; E. 717.12; F. 3.6; G. from top to bottom, left to right: 20.59, 8.02, 12.57, 3.95, 4.07, 8.5, 2.67, 1.28, 2,79, 5.71; H. 4; I. 7.8, 78, 780, 7,800; J. (7 × 1,000) + (6 × 10) + (2 × 1) + (8 × 1/10) + (9 × 1/100) + (1 × 1/1,000)

Week 14, Day 3 (page 71)
A. 2,500 pounds, 3 tons; B. trapezoid; C. seventy-five and two hundred thousandths, 7, 5, 2, 0, 0; (7 × 10) + (5 × 1) + (2 × 1/10); D. =; E. two hundred fifty-one and one hundred seventy-one thousandths; F. 800r5; G. 1/10 lb.; H. 2,489.85, 2,489.8, 2,000; I. >

Week 14, Day 4 (page 72)
A. 0.026; B. 8 c., 8 pt., 8 qt., 8 gal.; C. 3 × y; D. 2 1/6 c.; E. 1.08; F. >; G. 48, 60; H. 2, 5,000, 8,000, 9,000, 11,000; I. 981; J. 264

Week 15, Day 1 (page 73)
A. 30/8 = 3 3/4; B. 0.08; C. subtract 4; D. C; E. 293.7, 30, 18, 4,570, 25; F. (8 × 24) + (6 × 20); G. two hundred three and four hundred one thousandths; H. 99.999; I. 8, 8; J. 5.55

Week 15, Day 2 (page 74)
A. 500; B. 11, 110, 1,100; 12, 120, 1,200; 9, 90, 900; 8, 80, 800; C. 9/10, 0.9; D. 63,288, 60,000, 63,000, 63,300, 63,290; E. 47.68; F. 0.002; G. (2, 9); H. 14; I. 6, 12, 24, 48; J. 3 + (6 × 2) − 11 = 4

Week 15, Day 3 (page 75)
A. 0.4 + 0.02 = 0.42; B. All parallelograms are quadrilaterals. C. eighty-eight and ninety-six thousandths; 8, 8, 0, 9, 6; (8 × 10) + (8 × 1) + (9 × 1/100) + (6 × 1/1,000); D. 4; E. Check students' work. F. 1; G. Check students' work. 1, 0, 1, 1; H. 0.486; I. 5

Week 15, Day 4 (page 76)
A. 905.082; B. 2.47; C. 12; D. Davis, 1/8, 1 5/8; E. 1.27; F. >; G. 444.44; H. 58 yd., 204 sq. yd.; I. 67, 122; J. (2 × 6) ÷ 3

Week 16, Day 1 (page 77)
A. 36 in., 72 in.; B. 8.13; C. >; D. square, rectangle, rhombus, parallelogram; E. 0.3, 1.0, 3.2, 1.1, 0.9, 4.4, 6.2, 2.8; F. 3/4, 9/12, 18/24, 75/100, 15/20, 60/80, Finish; G. 88.023; H. 4,784; I. 84, 84; J. 99.7, 99.675, 99.99, 99.600, 99.601, 99.60

Week 16, Day 2 (page 78)
A. 83.1; B. 10 pack; C. 3, 2, (3, 2); 6, 4, (6, 4); 9, 6, (9, 6); 12, 8, (12, 8); D. 11:10; E. 3,680.46; F. 9.4; G. from top to bottom, left to right: 27.1, 13.15, 13.95, 6.5, 6.65, 7.3, 3.95, 2.55, 4.1, 3.2; H. 2,884.21, 2,884.2, 2,884, 2,880, 2,900, 3,000; I. 7,000, 700, 70, 7; J. 6

Week 16, Day 3 (page 79)
A. 10,000 g, 12 kg; B. 30 mi.; C. 54.31/fifty-four and thirty-one hundredths, 57.3/fifty-seven and three tenths, 54.7/fifty-four and seven tenths, 54.031/fifty-four and thirty-one thousandths, 57.03/fifty-seven and three hundredths, 54.003/fifty-four and three thousandths; D. <; E. distributive; F. 3,012r1; G. M; H. $9; I. >

Answer Key

Week 16, Day 4 (page 80)
A. largest: 100.3, smallest: 100.01; B. 5 g, 5 kg, 6,000 g, 100 kg; C. 360 ÷ s; D. 1/10;
E. 1 1/10; F. <; G. 990.2; H. 1, 3, 400, 700, 800; I. 7,104; J. 224

Week 17, Day 1 (page 81)
A. 21; B. 7.35; C. multiply by 3; D. rhombus, parallelogram; E. 424, 46, 12.7, 78.24, 239.0;
F. from bottom to top: 7.8 kg, 7.80 kg; 7.03 kg, 7.030 kg; 4.1 kg, 4.10 kg; 2.20 kg, 2.2 kg; G. sixty and three hundred thousandths; H. 6,793; I. 11, 11; J. 2.22

Week 17, Day 2 (page 82)
A. 700; B. 84, 840, 8,400; 121, 1,210, 12,100; 36, 360, 3,600; 28, 280, 2,800; C. 75/100, 0.75; D. 61,200, 60,000, 61,000, 61,200, 61,200; E. 1.74; F. 0.03; G. Check students' work. 16 units; H. 9; I. 4, 16, 64, 256;
J. 11 + (6 × 6) − 8 = 39

Week 17, Day 3 (page 83)
A. 0.78 + 0.1 = 0.88; B. 2,900; C. 11.1/eleven and one tenth, 11.01/eleven and one hundredth, 1.111/one and one hundred eleven thousandths, 1.01/one and one hundredth, 1.11/one and eleven hundredths, 11.11/eleven and eleven hundredths; D. 300; E. Check students' work.
F. 1/2; G. Check students' work. 15, 16, 14, 16;
H. 900.42; I. 2

Week 17, Day 4 (page 84)
A. 3,400.102; B. 11.67; C. hour; D. 2 1/4 mi.;
E. 1 16/100; F. >; G. 896; H. 15 ft., 11 sq. ft.;
I. 2,592; J. 90°

Week 18, Day 1 (page 85)
A. 30°; B. 8.59; C. =; D. Check students' work.
E. 0.7, 2.6, 1.4, 0.8, 0.9, 8.3, 5.5, 0.2; F. 1/4, 4/16, 25/100, 3/12, 5/20, 20/80, Finish;
G. 67.008; H. 480,000; I. 4, 4; J. 0.3, 0.5, 0.3, 0.7, 0.88, 0.210, 0.222

Week 18, Day 2 (page 86)
A. 419.20; B. 1 5/8; C. 2, 1, (2, 1); 4, 2, (4, 2); 6, 3, (6, 3); 8, 4, (8, 4); D. 4:00; E. 5.19; F. 3.8;
G. from top to bottom, left to right: 8.84, 5.16, 3.68, 2.63, 2.53, 1.15, 1.02, 1.61, 0.92, 0.23;
H. 2,694.65, 2,694.7, 2,695, 2,690, 2,700, 3,000; I. 48.79, 487.9, 4,879, 48,790;
J. (7 × 1,000) + (3 × 100) + (4 × 10) + (4 × 1/100) + (2 × 1/1,000)

Week 18, Day 3 (page 87)
A. 8 T., 15,500 lb.; B. 333 yd., 1 ft.; C. Check students' work. D. <; E. 3.5; F. 414r5; G. 5/7;
H. trapezoids; I. 28

Week 18, Day 4 (page 88)
A. 9.040; B. 8 mL, 5 L, 8 L, 9,000 mL;
C. 40 ÷ m; D. 1 hr. and 38 min.; E. 1 55/100;
F. =; G. 37.87; H. 1, 2, 6, 80, 100; I. 624;
J. 210

Week 19, Day 1 (page 89)
A. >, >, <; B. 16/3; C. subtract 3; D. 8, 8, 5, 5, 4, 4, 6, 6; E. 661, 110, 458, 772.6, 9.0;
F. from bottom to top: 15.8 kg, 15.80 kg; 15.1 kg, 15.10 kg; 15.08 kg, 15.080 kg; 15.01 kg, 15.010 kg; G. one and fifty-three thousandths;
H. 0.003; I. 7, 7; J. 2.5

Week 19, Day 2 (page 90)
A. 300; B. 12, 120, 1,200; 11, 110, 1,100; 4, 40, 400; 7, 70, 700; C. 2/5, 0.4; D. true, false;
E. 6,841.7; F. 500; G. Check students' work. 12 sq. units; H. 32°; I. 36, 48, 60, 72;
J. 3 × (12 − 6) + 4 = 22

Week 19, Day 3 (page 91)
A. 0.5 + 0.4 = 0.9; B. 2,460;
C. 22.03/twenty-two and three hundredths, 22.3/twenty-two and three tenths, 23.003/twenty-three and three thousandths, 22.003/twenty-two and three thousandths, 20.33/twenty and thirty-three hundredths, 23.23/twenty-three and twenty-three hundredths;
D. 256; E. Check students' work. F. 1/2;
G. Check students' work. 89, 89, 89, 90;
H. 0.071; I. 1

Answer Key

Week 19, Day 4 (page 92)
A. 210.73; B. 13.16; C. cup; D. 1/12;
E. 1 75/100; F. <; G. 1,603.4; H. 21 in.,
26 sq. in.; I. 63,035; J. 45°

Week 20, Day 1 (page 93)
A. 42°; B. 1,331; C. =; D. Check students' work.
E. 0, 1.4, 1.0, 1.1, 2.6, 4.8, 1.6, 3.3; F. 0.5,
40/80, 0.50, 6/12, 2/4, 0.500, Finish;
G. 20,400.19; H. 975; I. 7, 7; J. 0.375, 0.078,
0.022, 0.400, 0.004, 0.40, 0.388, 0.177

Week 20, Day 2 (page 94)
A. 1.5 inches shaded; B. 8 pies; C. 1, 5,
(1, 5); 2, 10, (2, 10): 3, 15, (3, 15); 4, 20,
(4, 20); D. 3:00; E. 7,661.65; F. 2 ones; G. 7,
37, 19, 23, 11, 17, 13, 31, 5, Finish; H. acute;
I. 111, 11.1, 1.11, 0.111; J. (2 × 100) + (3 × 1)
+ (2 × 1/100) + (8 × 1/1,000)

Week 20, Day 3 (page 95)
A. 1; B. 65,000; C. 8.78/eight and seventy-eight
hundredths, 87.8/eighty-seven and eight tenths,
808.7/eight hundred eight and seven tenths,
0.878/eight hundred seventy-eight thousandths,
87.87/eight-seven and eighty-seven hundredths;
80.78/eighty and seventy-eight hundredths; D. <;
E. commutative; F. 978r4; G. 15 min.; H. 0.27;
I. >

Week 20, Day 4 (page 96)
A. 1 1/3; B. 20 pt., 12 qt., 4 gal., 80 c.;
C. 2 × (8 − 1); D. Pokey, 1/20; E. 1 4/10; F. <;
G. 962.39; H. 3,000, 5,000, 6,000, 8,000,
10,000; I. 18,450; J. 16

Week 21, Day 1 (page 97)
A. 5/8, 11/12; B. 3.2; C. add 18; D. Check
students' work. E. 100, 300, 83.8, 966, 145;
F. from bottom to top: 0.55 kg, 0.550 kg;
0.25 kg, 0.250 kg; 0.2 kg, 0.20 kg; 0.05 kg,
0.050 kg; G. one thousand two and three
hundred nine thousandths; H. 110,000; I. 24,
24; J. 7.41

Week 21, Day 2 (page 98)
A. 2 1/4; B. 49, 490, 4,900; 24, 240, 2,400;
27, 270, 2,700; 16, 160, 1,600; C. 4/5, 0.8;
D. divide by 2; 16, 11; E. 20.52; F. 8; G. (7, 4);
H. arrow pointing up; I. 3,452.3;
J. 7 + (42 ÷ 6) × 2 = 28

Week 21, Day 3 (page 99)
A. 0.22 + 0.44 = 0.66; B. 5,000; C. Check
students' work. 2, 0, 6; D. 12; E. Check students'
work. F. 35; G. Check students' work. 100, 101,
99, 100; H. 13.004; I. 1

Week 21, Day 4 (page 100)
A. 3 × 3/4; B. 89.304 > 89.5; C. 36;
D. 27 5/6 mi.; E. 1,000, 200, 111, 61, 95; F. <;
G. 674.22; H. 20 2/3 mi., 22 sq. mi.; I. 7,236;
J. 6

Week 22, Day 1 (page 101)
A. 60°; B. 30, 60; C. =; D. Check students' work.
4, 4, opposite sides are parallel, all sides are
congruent; E. 1.2, 0.3, 2.5, 3.9, 3.2, 0.8, 6.4,
1.1; F. 10/50, 1/5, 2/10, 4/20, 8/40, 0.2,
Finish; G. 49.113; H. 0.234; I. 9, 9; J. 0.05,
0.07, 0.49, 0.50, 0.4, 0.10, 0.09, 0.33, 0.01

Week 22, Day 2 (page 102)
A. 1 1/3; B. 3,150; C. 3, 4, (3, 4); 6, 8,
(6, 8); 9, 12, (9, 12); 12, 16, (12, 16); D. 11:50;
E. 34.12; F. 1 1/6; G. 5; H. obtuse; I. 58.3,
583, 5,830, 58,300; J. (2 × 1,000) +
(2 × 100) + (5 × 10) + (3 × 1) + (2 × 1/100) +
(6 × 1/1,000)

Week 22, Day 3 (page 103)
A. 19,000 g, 18 kg; B. 7 × 1 = 7;
C. 9.89/nine and eighty-nine hundredths,
99.8/ninety-nine and eight tenths, 9.08/nine
and eight hundredths, 0.998/nine hundred
ninety-eight thousandths, 90.09/ninety and nine
hundredths, 9.09/nine and nine hundredths;
D. =; E. zero; F. 508; G. 1/4 lb.; H. >; I. <

Week 22, Day 4 (page 104)
A. 1/2; B. 1/2 yd., 36 in., 4 ft., 2 1/2 yd.;
C. 15 ÷ (2 + 3); D. 5/8; E. 2.24, 1.5, 7.675,
9.55; F. <; G. 264.46; H. 1,000, 3,000, 4,000,
7,000, 8,000; I. 40,896; J. 2.800 lb.

Week 23, Day 1 (page 105)
A. 300,000, 30,000,000, 300,000,000; B. 8.29;
C. multiply by 2; D. Check students' work.
E. 780, 68, 218.3, 909, 67.81; F. from bottom
to top: 41.11 kg, 41.110 kg; 41.1 kg, 41.10 kg;
4.11 kg, 4.110 kg; 4.01 kg, 4.010 kg; G. eight
thousand three hundred seven and three tenths;
H. 73; I. 16, 16; J. 6.1

Answer Key

Week 23, Day 2 (page 106)
A. 1 4/5; B. 7, 70, 700; 12, 120, 1,200; 9, 90, 900; 4, 40 400; C. 43,281, 40,000, 43,000, 43,300, 4 ,280; D. $x \div 3 = y$, 24, 36; E. 28; F. 60; G. 1, 2); H. arrow pointing down; I. 34.52 ; J. $8 \times 4 + (8 \div 2) = 36$

Week 23, Day 3 (page 107)
A. $0.01 + 0.11 = 0.12$; B. 5; C. Check students' work. 1,140; E. Check students' work. F. 1; G. Check students' work. 9, 7, 8, 10; H. 9, 7, 8, 10; H 21.95; I. 5

Week 23, Day 4 (page 108)
A. 1 4 × 2/3; B. 0.4 = 0.404; C. 60; D. yes, Answers will vary. E. 7.9, 12.5, 22.25, 1.7; F. < G. 32,080.63; H. 23 1/3 ft., 26 sq. ft.; I. 1 ,266; J. 4,752

Week 24, Day 1 (page 109)
A. 85°; B. 5.28; C. <; D. obtuse; E. 0.6, 2.0, 1, 0.3, 0.9, 2.3, 3.1, 4.2; F. 0.25, 1/4, 4/16, /12, 0.250, 5/20, Finish; G. 52.38; I. 96,000,000; I. 8, 8; J. 12, 6, 3; 3, 4, 12; 4, 5, 9

Week 24, Day 2 (page 110)
A. 2; B. 71; C. 1, 6, (1, 6); 2, 12, (2, 12); 3, 18, (3, 18); 4, 24, (4, 24); D. 8:15; E. 152.74; F. 8.7; G. 0; H. right; I. 9,870, 987, 98.7, 9.87; J. $(3 \times 1,000) + (5 \times 1) + (3 \times 1/10) + (1 \times 1/100) + (9 \times 1/1,000)$

Week 24, Day 3 (page 111)
A. 8 T., 16,000 lb.; B. $(45 - 15) \div 3$; C. 7.77/seven and seventy-seven hundredths, 0.777/seven hundred seventy-seven thousandths, 7.7/seven and seven tenths, 77.7/seventy-seven and seven tenths, 77.77/seventy-seven and seventy-seven hundredths, 0.77/seventy-seven hundredths; D. <; E. 1/16; F. 923; G. 7 1/3 oz., 7 oz; H. =; I. >

Week 24, Day 4 (page 112)
A. 16; B. 1 1/2 lb., 1 T., 2,200 lb., 3,500 lb.; C. $156 - b$; D. 1/12; E. 18.25, 4.5, 6.8, 10.05; F. <; G. $505.61; H. 1,000, 2, 4,000, 5, 10; I. 109,648; J. 84.4°F

Week 25, Day 1 (page 113)
A. 1/2, 3/8; 37,620; C. multiply by 10; D. Check students' work. 3, 3, three equal sides, three equal angles; E. 120, 600, 81, 82.2, 9,880; F. from bottom to top: 8/10 kg, 4/5 kg; 2/3 kg, 4/6 kg; 15/25 kg, 3/5 kg; 3/9 kg, 1/3 kg; G. eight hundred two and two hundred three thousandths; H. 7.895; I. 6, 6; J. 0.6

Week 25, Day 2 (page 114)
A. 1 1/2; B. 40, 400, 4,000; 36, 360, 3,600; 63, 630, 6,300; 48, 480, 4,800; C. 60; D. +10, 18; E. 16.23; F. 0.1; G. (3, 1); H. arrow pointing right; I. 783.62; J. 4

Week 25, Day 3 (page 115)
A. $0.55 - 0.08 = 0.47$; B. 0.07; C. 16 ÷ 2; D. 0.1 L; E. Check students' work. F. 1/2; G. Check students' work. 3, 1, 3, 1; H. 100.27; I. 4

Week 25, Day 4 (page 116)
A. 4/4 × 7/5; B. 78.8 < 78.708; C. 1,000; D. 1/2 lb.; E. 3.5, 6.75, 5.25, 12.4; F. <; G. 2,919.13; H. 27 1/2 ft., 39 sq. ft.; I. 2,968; J. 6:15

Week 26, Day 1 (page 117)
A. 3/8, 3/16; B. 1.84; C. <; D. Answers will vary. E. 4/8, 2/4, 9/18, 10/20, 3/6, 7/14; F. 1/10, 10/100, 2/20, 5/50, 0.1, 0.10, Finish; G. 80,400.009; H. 111,111; I. 9, 9; J. 3, 9; 3, 6, 7; 7, 3, 9

Week 26, Day 2 (page 118)
A. 4/5; B. No, they only had 384. C. 6, 3, (6, 3); 12, 6, (12, 6); 18, 9, (18, 9); 24, 12, (24, 12); D. 3:50; E. 85.44; F. 1.8; G. 200, 500, 500, 200, 1,920; H. straight; I. 96.51, 9,651, 96,510, 965,100; J. $(2 \times 100) + (6 \times 10) + (7 \times 1) + (8 \times 1/10) + (7 \times 1/1,000)$

Week 26, Day 3 (page 119)
A. 12,000 g, 12 kg; B. 0.600; C. 2, 2, 5; D. >; E. identity; F. 737r6; G. 16 in.; H. <; I. <

Week 26, Day 4 (page 120)
A. 6 mi.; B. 500 mL, 1 L, 2,500 mL, 3 L; C. $14 + p$; D. 5 3/4 c.; E. 9.5, 7.25, 11.11, 13.8; F. <; G. $524.66; H. 9, 5, 21, 27, 11; I. 2,926; J. $115

Answer Key

Week 27, Day 1 (page 121)
A. 1/2, 11/15; B. 25,133; C. divide by 10;
D. Check students' work. 4, 4, one set of opposite
parallel sides; E. 212.0, 341.12, 67.9, 78, 9;
F. from bottom to top: 4/6 kg, 8/12 kg; 5/10 kg,
3/6 kg; 1/5 kg, 5/25 kg; 10/100 kg,
1/10 kg; G. four and eight hundred twenty-nine
thousandths; H. 0.898; I. 8, 8; J. 18.6

Week 27, Day 2 (page 122)
A. 6/7; B. 8, 80, 800; 6, 60, 600; 7, 70, 700;
6, 60, 600; C. 50,652, 50,000, 51,000, 50,700,
50,650; D. $x \times 5 = y$, 25; E. 629.71; F. 0.07;
G. (3, 0); H. arrow pointing left; I. 678.032;
J. 8

Week 27, Day 3 (page 123)
A. Check students' work. B. 1.07; C. 6, 2, 4;
D. 0.28 g; E. Check students' work. F. 1;
G. Check students' work. 43, 41, 43, 42;
H. 0.486; I. 1

Week 27, Day 4 (page 124)
A. largest: 111.48, smallest: 111.4; B. 12,000;
C. km; D. Stop 'n Go, 4/15; E. 27.3, 5.25,
18.08, 27.057; F. >; G. 1,279.2; H. 19 in.,
21 sq. in.; I. 1,960; J. 117

Week 28, Day 1 (page 125)
A. 5/8, 1/6; B. 8.28; C. >; D. Check students'
work. 3, 3, two sides are equal lengths; E. 2/8,
4/16, 10/40, 3/12; 9/36; F. 2/3, 12/18,
10/15, 20/30, 16/24, 200/300; G. 231.5;
H. 9,000,000; I. 144, 144; J. 9, 3, 6; 8, 2, 4; 2,
4, 8

Week 28, Day 2 (page 126)
A. 1 3/5; B. 18 rows, Answers will vary.
C. 0, 2, (0, 2); 0, 4, (0, 4); 0, 6, (0, 6); 0, 8,
(0, 8); D. 7:25; E. 912.44; F. 4.3; G. 600, 300,
600, 300, 2,106; H. 33°; I. 71,000, 710, 71,
7.1; J. $(8 \times 100) + (3 \times 10) + (1 \times 1/10) +$
$(2 \times 1/100) + (2 \times 1/1,000)$

Week 28, Day 3 (page 127)
A. 17,000 lb., 8.5 T.; B. 3/4, 9/12; C. 4, 3, 5,
60; D. <; E. $9 \times 1 = 9$; F. 833r1; G. 1 1/3 lb.;
H. <; I. <

Week 28, Day 4 (page 128)
A. 20 min.; B. 1,000 mm, 10,000 cm,
200 m, 1.5 km; C. $3 \times z + 18$; D. 5/6 in.; E. 6.4,
29.060, 14.5, 2.43; F. >; G. 1.25; H. 1, 3, 48,
72, 120; I. 441; J. $204.36

Week 29, Day 1 (page 129)
A. 12 5/8, 3 7/8; B. 28,440; C. divide by 8;
D. rectangle and rhombus, square; E. 118,
90, 903, 300, 732; F. 720 cubic in.; G. four
thousand five hundred eight and five hundred
eight thousandths; H. 29.384; I. 132, 132; J. 12

Week 29, Day 2 (page 130)
A. 1 1/3; B. 144, 1,440, 14,400; 132, 1,320,
13,200; 80, 800, 8,000; 81, 810, 8,100;
C. 58,539, 60,000, 59,000, 58,500, 58,540;
D. box A, Answers will vary. E. 0.29; F. 0.003;
G. (3, 6); H. 8 ÷ 7, 8/7 = 1 1/7; I. 18,020; J. 6

Week 29, Day 3 (page 131)
A. 0.7 − 0.33 = 0.37; B. pentagon; C. 4, 4, 4,
64 cubic units; D. 15,000; E. Check students'
work. F. 1; G. Check students' work. 68, 67, 68,
67; H. 71.03; I. 1

Week 29, Day 4 (page 132)
A. $2 \times 1/5$; B. 5.6 > 5.600; C. two; D. 3 5/12;
E. 7.004, 62.6, 5.25, 40.01; F. <; G. 1,853.27;
H. 20 2/3 m, 23 1/3 sq. m; I. 992; J. 1,420 mL

Week 30, Day 1 (page 133)
A. 9 1/4, 1/2; B. 5.94; C. <; D. Check students'
work. 3, 3, all three sides are unequal; E. 3/9,
6/18, 10/30, 2/6, 7/21, 4/12; F. 4/5, 40/50,
8/10, 400/500, 0.8, 0.80, Finish; G. 8.405;
H. 0.589; I. 8, 8; J. 6, 3, 2; 8, 2; 2, 3, 4, 6

Week 30, Day 2 (page 134)
A. 1 2/3; B. 4 1/5 sq. cm; C. 2, 0, (2, 0); 4, 0,
(4, 0); 6, 0, (6, 0); 8, 0, (8, 0); D. 7:40; E. 25.6;
F. 1.3; G. 300, 400, 400, 300, 1,904; H. 4 ÷ 5,
4/5; I. 0.898, 89.8, 898, 8,980; J. 1/6

Week 30, Day 3 (page 135)
A. It will be less since the other factor is less than
1. B. 15/45, 1/3; C. 84 cubic ft.; D. >; E. 4 × 3
= 3 × 4; F. 5r1; G. 1 min. 15 sec.; H. 3 5/6; I. >

Answer Key

Week 30, Day 4 (page 136)
A. 7/8; B. 1 1/2; C. *n* × 8; D. 5/8; E. 6 cubic units; F. >; G. 1,850.98; H. 591 1/6 mi.; I. 7,680; J. 1.1

Week 31, Day 1 (page 137)
A. Answers will vary. B. 16,281; C. add 1; D. equilateral; E. 70, 240, 778.35, 910, 8,002; F. from bottom to top: 9/9 kg, 3/3 kg; 2/3 kg, 24/36 kg; 50/100 kg, 7/14 kg; 1/8 kg, 8/64 kg; G. five hundred fifty-five and fifty-five hundredths; H. 10,000; I. 3, 3; J. 60.3

Week 31, Day 2 (page 138)
A. 1/12; B. 12, 120, 1,200; 11, 110, 1,100; 10, 100, 1,000; 9, 90, 900; C. 90,345, 90,000, 90,000, 90,300, 90,350; D. 7, 13, 8, 15; E. 3.6; F. 0.08; G. Check students' work. H. 4 ÷ 3, 4/3 = 1 1/3; I. 3.3; J. 48

Week 31, Day 3 (page 139)
A. 0.9 − 0.36 = 0.54; B. 0 and 1/2; C. 60 cubic cm; D. 3,700; E. Check students' work. F. 1; G. Check students' work. 100, 101, 102, 101; H. 25.409; I. 6

Week 31, Day 4 (page 140)
A. 2.1 × 4.2; B. 320; C. cm; D. 1 hr. 25 min.; E. 7 cubic units; F. <; G. 534.06; H. 3/4; I. 437; J. 24 sq. cm

Week 32, Day 1 (page 141)
A. 1/20; B. 7.76; C. <; D. Check students' work. Because the sides and angles are not equal. E. 4/6, 6/9, 12/18, 20/30, 8/12, 14/21; F. 4/10, 2/5, 0.4, 12/30, 20/50, 0.400, Finish; G. 50.66; H. 100; I. 81, 81; J. 4, 8; 6, 2, 3; 4, 5, 8

Week 32, Day 2 (page 142)
A. 1/4; B. 14 7/8; C. 4, 2, (4, 2); 8, 4, (8, 4); 12, 6, (12, 6); 16, 8, (16, 8); D. 11:20; E. 7; F. 4.7; G. 700, 200, 700, 200, 2,100; H. 1/12; I. 11,010, 110.1, 11.01, 1.101; J. 1/10

Week 32, Day 3 (page 143)
A. 168 cubic in.; B. 2/3 > 3/5; C. 108 cubic in.; D. <; E. 7,600, 22,800, 159,600; F. 179; G. 7/8; H. 408.008; I. =

Week 32, Day 4 (page 144)
A. 1 1/2 hr.; B. 8,000.016; C. 2*n* + 5; D. 4/15; E. 9 cubic units; F. =; G. 434.96; H. 1, 36, 60, 7, 120; I. 1,505; J. 11.70

Week 33, Day 1 (page 145)
A. 1/6; B. 13,150; C. add 2/8; D. Answers will vary. E. 7,853, 700, 87.4, 13, 90; F. from bottom to top: 0.8 kg, 8/10 kg; 0.5 kg, 5/10 kg; 3/10 kg, 0.30 kg; 1/4 kg, 0.25 kg; G. nine thousand eight hundred four and nine hundred eighty-seven thousandths; H. 5,984,500; I. 9, 9; J. 72.3

Week 33, Day 2 (page 146)
A. 1/5; B. 35, 350, 3,500; 44, 440, 4,400; 72, 720, 7,200; 108, 1,080, 10,800; C. 125,400, 130,000, 125,000, 125,400, 125,400; D. 8, 4, 22, 18; E. 13.3; F. 0.07; G. Check students' work. H. 24; I. 5,000; J. 9

Week 33, Day 3 (page 147)
A. 0.44 − 0.06 = 0.38; B. foot; C. 8 cubic cm, 60 cubic cm; D. 130,000; E. Check students' work. 15/16; F. 1; G. Check students' work. 80, 81, 79, 80, H. 8.8; I. 3

Week 33, Day 4 (page 148)
A. 87.5 × 0.66; B. 82,000; C. 108; D. 5/12; E. 6 cubic units; F. >; G. 57.88; H. 11 1/2 ft., 5 5/8 cubic ft.; I. 2,911; J. 14

Week 34, Day 1 (page 149)
A. 14; B. 1.37; C. <; D. Check students' work. 4, 4, opposite sides are parallel; E. 3/4, 4/5, 1/6, 5/6, 2/3, 1/2; F. 9/15, 6/10, 0.60, 3/5, 12/20, 30/50; G. 72.805; H. 7,500; I. 5, 5; J. 3, 7; 9, 5, 3; 1, 2, 5

Week 34, Day 2 (page 150)
A. 3/10; B. 13 1/5 sq. in.; C. 1, 1, (1, 1); 2, 2, (2, 2); 3, 3, (3, 3); 4, 4, (4, 4); D. 7:25; E. 3.6; F. 10.8; G. 1,728 cubic ft., 288 cubic ft., 2,016 cubic ft.; H. 12; I. 0.211, 21.1, 211, 2,110; J. 3

Week 34, Day 3 (page 151)
A. 0.47 − 0.28 = 0.19; B. The product is less than both factors. C. Answers will vary. D. <; E. 125 cubic in.; F. 30r8; G. 3/5; H. area, volume; I. =

Answer Key

Week 34, Day 4 (page 152)
A. 3/8; B. largest: 607.333, smallest: 607.03;
C. (50 – 5) ÷ 9; D. 1/20; E. 9 cubic units;
F. >; G. 976.05; H. 4, 3, 20, 6, 40; I. 1,944;
J. 3 in.

Week 35, Day 1 (page 153)
A. 24/25; B. 30,600; C. add 0.04; D. Check
students' work. E. 5, 4, 7, 1, 3, 6, 10, 1.5;
F. from bottom to top: 4/5 kg, 0.80 kg; 3/4 kg,
0.75 kg; 7/10 kg, 0.70 kg; 0.50 kg,
10/20 kg; G. three hundred two thousand twenty
and twenty-seven thousandths; H. 528.092;
I. 11, 11; J. 1.97

Week 35, Day 2 (page 154)
A. 1/20; B. 7, 70, 700; 11, 110, 1,100; 12,
120, 1,200; 9, 90, 900; C. 4,400.64, 4,000,
4,400, 4,400, 4,400.6; D. 4, 8, 16; E. 14.4;
F. 100; G. Check students' work. H. 12; I. 0.78;
J. z = 6

Week 35, Day 3 (page 155)
A. 0.82 – 0.2 = 0.62; B. ten thousands; neither,
they're equal; C. neither, they both have a
volume of 12 sq. units; D. 32; E. Check students'
work. F. 1; G. Check students' work. 12, 12, 12,
13; H. 970.18; I. 2

Week 35, Day 4 (page 156)
A. 8.54 × 0.13; B. 680; C. 5,280; D. 5;
E. 8 cubic units; F. >; G. 1,716.79; H. V = 3 × 2
× 6; I. 378; J. 105

Week 36, Day 1 (page 157)
A. 2 4/25; B. 6,946; C. >; D. right; E. 5/4, 2/1,
8/4, 12/6, 4/2, 8/7, 3/2; F. Answers will vary.
G. 1.003; H. 400,050; I. 72, 72; J. 7, 8, 2; 4, 3,
8, 6; 5, 3, 9

Week 36, Day 2 (page 158)
A. 1/2; B. 28 1/3; C. 4, 1, (4, 1); 8, 2, (8, 2);
12, 3 (12, 3); 16, 4, (16, 4); D. 6:05; E. 49.6;
F. 10.4; G. 1,950 min., 117,000 sec.; H. 3/16;
I. 304,000, 3,040, 304, 30.4; J. 6

Week 36, Day 3 (page 159)
A. 7 T., 14,200 lb.; B. 642.305; C. Answers will
vary. D. <; E. 2 2/3; F. 724; G. 3/4;
H. 14,000.20; I. >

Week 36, Day 4 (page 160)
A. 11,005.02; B. largest: 54.48, smallest: 44.54;
C. (12 × 5) – 8; D. 1/6; E. 9 cubic units; F. <;
G. 11.95; H. 1, 2, 16, 18, 10; I. 3,612;
J. about 75 sq. ft.

Week 37, Day 1 (page 161)
A. 24/35; B. 2.4; C. add 0.25; D. Check
students' work. 4, 4, one set of opposite sides is
parallel; E. 61, 5,560, 80, 39.25, 5.99;
F. from bottom to top: 5 kg, 5/1 kg; 4/4 kg,
1 kg; 0.5 kg, 500/1,000 kg; 2/5 kg, 0.4 kg;
G. seven hundred seventy-seven and two hundred
thousandths; H. 4,000,000; I. 12, 12; J. 5.69

Week 37, Day 2 (page 162)
A. 5/9; B. 24, 240, 2,400; 96, 960, 9,600; 30,
300, 3,000; 55, 550, 5,500; C. 293.248, 300,
290, 293.2, 293.25; D. 9, 12; E. 27.6;
F. 70,000; G. A (4,2), B (2,3), C (2,0), D (1,5),
E (4, 0); H. 1/16; I. 34,010; J. m = 12

Week 37, Day 3 (page 163)
A. 7.5 cubic yd.; B. 3/4; C. h = 8 in.; D. 14;
E. Check students' work. F. 1/2; G. Check
students' work. 48, 48, 49, 48; H. 13.04; I. 6

Week 37, Day 4 (page 164)
A. 0.544 × 0.94; B. 0.423; C. km; D. 5/12;
E. 11 cubic units; F. <; G. 94.29; H. 17 2/3 mi.,
15 5/6 mi.; I. 3,750; J. $0.15;

Week 38, Day 1 (page 165)
A. 2; B. 50,490; C. >; D. trapezoid, 4, 1, 0;
E. 3/4, 3/5, 2/3, 4/6, 7/8, 5/7; F. 1/6, 7/42,
3/18, 8/48, 2/12, 5/30, 10/60, 11/66, Finish;
G. 17.089; H. 837,470; I. 8, 8; J. 6, 3, 4; 8, 2;
6, 3, 9

Week 38, Day 2 (page 166)
A. 3/8; B. 114 1/3 sq. mi.; C. 5, 4, (5, 4); 10,
8, (10, 8); 15, 12 (15, 12); 20, 16, (20, 16); D.
204; E. 68.67; F. 0.6; G. Check students' work.
Yes, she has practiced 10 1/2 hours total. H. 6;
I. 3.456, 345.6, 3,456, 34,560; J. 1/8

Week 38, Day 3 (page 167)
A. 20,000 g, 19.5 kg; B. 10.238; C. Answers
will vary. D. <; E. 5; F. 186; G. 2/3; H,
642.007; I. 80

Answer Key

Week 38, Day 4 (page 168)
A. 1.2 × 1.837; B. 9,760; C. (6 + 7) × 3;
D. 13 1/4; E. 12 cubic units; F. <; G. $841.62;
H. 9, 15, 21, 24, 30; I. 546; J. $78.00

Week 39, Day 1 (page 169)
A. 6 7/8; B. 5.27; C. add 2/6; D. hexagon, 6,
3 sets, 0; E. 78.6, 8,900, 908.2, 88, 83.3; F.
from bottom to top: 2.5 kg, 250/100 kg; 4/2 kg,
2 kg; 3/5 kg, 0.6 kg; 4/16 kg, 250/1000 kg;
G. two hundred twenty-two thousand fifty and
thirty-eight thousandths; H. 0.007; I. 96, 96;
J. 33.3

Week 39, Day 2 (page 170)
A. 3/32; B. 3, 30, 300; 8, 80, 800; 5, 50, 500;
11, 110, 1,100; C. 292.942, 300, 290, 292.9,
292.94; D. 6, 12, 8; E. 71.04; F. eight tenths;
G. A (3, 3), B (2, 1), C (5, 5), D (1, 2), E (0, 5);
H. 1 1/4 mi.; I. 0.33; J. $a = 23$

Week 39, Day 3 (page 171)
A. 0.6 − 0.52 = 0.08; B. 21; C. (8 × 4 × 3) +
(4 × 4 × 3); D. 57; E. Check students' work.
F. 0; G. Check students' work. 19, 17, 19, 20;
H. 670.021; I. 10

Week 39, Day 4 (page 172)
A. largest: 81.111, smallest: 81.001;
B. $1000 ÷ e; C. mm; D. Kate, 1 1/8;
E. 12 cubic units; F. <; G. 88.85; H. 16, 32, 48,
96, 10; I. 1,045; J. 396 sq. ft.

Week 40, Day 1 (page 173)
A. 4 7/8; B. 3.39; C. <; D. rectangle, 4, 2 sets,
4; E. 1/6, 1/4, 3/7, 3/9, 1/3, 1/5; F. 12/32,
6/16, 15/40, 3/8, 18/48, 9/24, Finish;
G. 5,042.035; H. 67,000; I. 6, 6; J. 7, 3, 2, 6;
7, 4; 3, 5

Week 40, Day 2 (page 174)
A. 600; B. 9 3/8 sq. ft.; C. 6, 4, (6, 4); 12, 8,
(12, 8); 18, 12, (18, 12); 24, 16, (24, 16);
D. 7:27; E. 68.67; F. 10.1; G. 800, 800, 800,
800, 3,312; H. 7/15; I. 990,000, 9,900, 990,
99; J. 6

Week 40, Day 3 (page 175)
A. 1 1/12; B. 4; C. Answers will vary. D. >;
E. 16; F. 78; G. 40 min.; H. 81.05; I. 1/16

Week 40, Day 4 (page 176)
A. 2.111 × 7.2; B. 9.872; C. 7 × n − 5; D. 1 hr.
25 min.; E. 15 cubic units; F. <; G. 434.46; H. 3,
5, 14,000, 18,000, 20,000; I. 2,904; J. 5